Homelessness

ISSUES

Volume 130

Series Editor

Lisa Firth

Independence

Educational Publishers
Cambridge

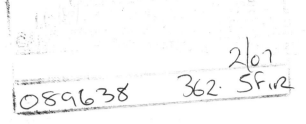

First published by Independence
PO Box 295
Cambridge CB1 3XP
England

British Library Cataloguing in Publication Data
Homelessness – (Issues Series)
I. Firth, Lisa II. Series
362.5'0941

ISBN 978 1 86168 376 2

Printed in Great Britain
MWL Print Group Ltd

Cover
The illustration on the front cover is by
Angelo Madrid.

CONTENTS

Introduction

Homelessness is the one hundred and thirtieth volume in the **Issues** series. The aim of this series is to offer up-to-date information about important issues in our world.

Homelessness looks at the major issues surrounding homelessness, homeless young people, and solutions to the homelessness problem.

The information comes from a wide variety of sources and includes:
Government reports and statistics
Newspaper reports and features
Magazine articles and surveys
Website material
Literature from lobby groups
and charitable organisations.

It is hoped that, as you read about the many aspects of the issues explored in this book, you will critically evaluate the information presented. It is important that you decide whether you are being presented with facts or opinions. Does the writer give a biased or an unbiased report? If an opinion is being expressed, do you agree with the writer?

Homelessness offers a useful starting-point for those who need convenient access to information about the many issues involved. However, it is only a starting-point. Following each article is a URL to the relevant organisation's website, which you may wish to visit for further information.

* * * * *

What is homelessness?

Information from Crisis

In its broadest sense homelessness is the problem faced by people who lack a place to live that is supportive, affordable, decent and secure. Whilst rough sleepers are the most visible homeless population, the vast majority of homeless people live in hostels, squats, bed and breakfasts or in temporary and insecure conditions with friends and family.[1]

Whilst there is some debate over the precise definition of homelessness there is a widespread acceptance that homelessness is about more than rooflessness

People who experience homelessness are often amongst the most vulnerable people in our society, suffering from a combination of poor housing, unemployment, low income, bad health, poor skills, loneliness, isolation and relationship breakdown.

Whilst there is some debate over the precise definition of homelessness there is a widespread acceptance that homelessness is about more than rooflessness. A home is not just a physical space; it provides 'roots, identity, security, a sense of belonging and a place of emotional wellbeing'.[2] It is also a practical prerequisite to living and working in modern society, with a permanent address often being a basic requirement for employers and other essential services.

In United Kingdom homelessness is most commonly defined and discussed in terms of Homelessness Legislation, the first of which was

Fighting for hope for homeless people

introduced as the Housing (homeless persons) Act in 1977.[3] Whilst the legal definition of homelessness is pitched in broad terms those who are actually accepted as homeless (the statutory homeless) and eligible for support by local authorities are a much narrower group. Those who are not clearly entitled to support are largely single people (people without dependants) they are the Hidden Homeless.

The legal definition of homelessness

A household is legally homeless if, either, they do not have accommodation that they are entitled to occupy, which is accessible and physically available to them or, they have accommodation but it is not reasonable for them to continue to occupy this accommodation.[4]

This definition is much wider than rough sleeping.

Statutory homelessness

Statutory homelessness refers to those homeless people or households who are recognised by local authorities to be homeless and are therefore recognised in government homeless statistics.

Homeless households

⇨ a family or individual who has applied for local authority housing support and been judged to be homeless. Local authority homeless statistics are based on households, not individuals.

Homeless families

⇨ people with dependent children

⇨ Having a dependent child is the most common reason for being accepted as in priority need by local authorities.

⇨ Between January and March 2005, in 51% of priority need acceptances, the presence of dependent children in the household was the primary reason for priority need. A further 12 per cent of households had priority need because they included a pregnant woman.

Single homeless

⇨ individuals or couples without dependants.
⇨ traditionally helped by Crisis.
⇨ no one has to find them accommodation, except in specific cases of vulnerability such as physical or mental health problems.
⇨ Crisis estimates that there are around 380,000 hidden single homeless people in Great Britain. This includes those staying in hostels, B&Bs, squats, on friends' floors and in overcrowded accommodation (Crisis, *How Many, How Much?* 2003).
⇨ Government street counts estimate 502 people sleeping outside in England on any one night, 289 of which are in Greater London (DCLG, June 2006).

Crisis estimates that there are around 380,000 hidden single homeless people in Great Britain, including those staying in hostels, B&Bs, squats, on friends' floors and overcrowded accommodation

---

There are three categories of statutory homelessness:
⇨ Unintentionally homeless and in priority need.
⇨ Intentionally homeless and in priority need.
⇨ Homeless but not in priority need.

A local authority must consider all applications for housing assistance and investigate if an applicant is homeless or threatened with homelessness; if they are in priority need; if they are intentionally homeless; and if necessary if they have a local connection.

Priority need

Under the homeless legislation certain categories of homeless household are considered to have priority need for accommodation. Priority need applies to families with dependent children, and households that include someone who is vulnerable due to pregnancy, old age, physical disability, mental illness or domestic violence. In 2002 the priority need categories were expanded to include homeless 16- and 17-year-olds, care leavers aged 18, 19 and 20, people who are vulnerable because of time spent in care, the armed forces, prison or custody and people who are vulnerable because of violence.

If a household is considered to be in priority need and homeless through no fault of their own then local authorities have a duty to ensure that suitable accommodation is available for them. The accommodation may be provided in local authority housing stock, or can arrange for it to be provided by a housing association or registered social landlord or a landlord in the private sector. This accommodation must be made available until the household has found a settled home, until the household voluntarily leaves the accommodation provided (i.e. they find their own accommodation or accept tenancy with a private landlord), or a suitable tenancy is allocated in an authority's housing stock.

If permanent housing is not available for successful applicants due to a shortage of social housing or current vacancies then they will have to wait in temporary accommodation.

Intentionally homeless

This is when a household is considered to have brought homelessness on themselves through a deliberate action or omission (non-action) unless they were not aware of a relevant fact. This may be due to someone deciding to leave their previous accommodation even though it would have been reasonable for them to occupy it, or because loss of tenancy or eviction is due to non-payment of rent or anti-social behaviour.

Under the 1996 Act if someone is found to be homeless, eligible for assistance but intentionally homeless temporary accommodation must be secured for them for a period that will 'give them a reasonable chance of finding accommodation for themselves', which may only be for 28 days. For those without priority need temporary accommodation does not need to be provided, but the local authority must ensure that they get advice and assistance to help them get accommodation for themselves.[5]

Local connection

You have local connection with an area if either you, or someone you might reasonably be expected to live with, have a connection based upon:
1) present or past normal residence in that area or
2) employment in that area or
3) family associations or
4) other special reasons.

The current duty on local authorities is to house people who are considered to be 'homeless' or

Homeless households in priority need

Homeless households in priority need accepted by local authorities, by priority need category, England, 2006 (quarter 2). Provisional data.

Category	%
Household with dependent children	55%
Household member pregnant	12%
Household member vulnerable through old age	2%
Household member vulnerable through physical disability	5%
Household member vulnerable through mental illness	8%
Household member vulnerable through young person	8%
Household member vulnerable through domestic violence	4%
Household member vulnerable through other	6%
Homeless in emergency	0%

Source: DCLG P1E Homelessness returns (quarterly). Crown copyright.

502 people are sleeping outside in England on any one night

'threatened with homelessness' (if it is likely they will become homeless within 28 days), provided that: they are in a 'priority need' category, that they did not become homeless intentionally, and that they have a 'connection' with the area of the local authority.

Those people who usually do not fall into this group and have no clear statutory right to housing are essentially single people and couples without children. The term 'single homeless people' is usually used to describe this group of people.

Hidden homelessness

Hidden homelessness is the problem of single homeless people who exist out of sight in hostels, bed and breakfasts, and squats or with friends and family.

The nature of the legislation in Britain means that despite often being extremely vulnerable, many single people are denied access to appropriate support and housing. As a consequence not everyone who is homeless receives housing from their local authority, some are refused assistance, others are unaware of their entitlements, some do not bother applying because their entitlements are so slight and some are too vulnerable to look for help.

These homeless people are therefore not identified by government homeless statistics, and are hidden from view.

Crisis campaigns to raise awareness of the plight of Hidden Homeless people and has published a series of reports on the causes and consequences of this problem.

Rough sleeping in England

Rough sleeping, England, 1998-2004.

Source: Office of the Deputy Prime Minister. Crown copyright.

Notes

1 ODPM (2002) *More Than A Roof, A report into tackling homelessness*, p1

Hidden homelessness is the problem of single homeless people who exist out of sight in hostels, bed and breakfasts, and squats or with friends and family

2 Warnes A, Crane M, Whitehead, N and Fu R (2003) *Homelessness Factfile*, Crisis p2
3 Burrow, Pleace & Quilgars (1997) *Homelessness & Social Policy* p3
4 Kenway & Palmer (2003) *How Many, How Much*, Crisis, New Policy Institute p2
5 Homelessness Code of Guidance for Local Authorities (2002) http://www.odpm.gov.uk/embedded_object.asp?id=1149852

⇨ Crisis is the national charity for single homeless people. Its mission is to fight homelessness and empower people to fulfil their potential and transform their lives. For more information, please visit the Crisis website at www.crisis.org.uk

© Crisis

Factors which increase risk of homelessness

Institutionalisation
⇨ time in local authority care
⇨ contact with the criminal justice system
⇨ previous service in the Armed Forces

Health
⇨ alcohol and drug misuse
⇨ mental health problems, including mental illness and personality disorders
⇨ a combination of mental health, drug and alcohol problems
⇨ experience of physical or sexual abuse

Relationship breakdown
⇨ disputes with parents or step-parents
⇨ marital or relationship breakdown
⇨ domestic violence
⇨ bereavement

⇨ lack of social support networks

Education and work
⇨ learning difficulties and literacy problems
⇨ exclusion from school
⇨ lack of qualifications
⇨ unemployment

Housing
⇨ housing shortage, in some areas
⇨ imbalance in supply and demand for housing

Others
⇨ previous experience of homelessness
⇨ debt, especially rent or mortgage arrears
⇨ benefit problems

The average time between the triggers that lead to homelessness and when homelessness finally occurs is nine years (*Routes into Homelessness*, Centre for the Analysis of Social Exclusion, 2000).

A brief history of homelessness

Information from St Mungo's

For as long as historical records have been kept, Britain has had a homelessness problem. As far back as the 7th century, the English king Hlothaere passed laws to punish vagrants. William the Conqueror forbade anyone to leave the land where he worked. Edward the First ordered weekly searches to round up vagrants.

For as long as historical records have been kept, Britain has had a homelessness problem

---

The numbers of vagrants has risen and fallen, and precise figures are hard to come by, but we know that 16th-century estimates put the numbers of vagrants at 20,000 or more. And it was in the 16th century that the state first tried to house vagrants rather than punish them. It began introducing bridewells, places meant to take vagrants in and train them for a profession – in reality dirty and brutal places. By the 18th century workhouses replaced the bridewells, but these were intended to discourage over-reliance on state help; at best they were spartan places with meagre food and sparse furnishings – at worst they were insanitary and uncaring places.

The successor to the workhouse was the spike (dormitory housing provided by local boroughs), which was familiar to George Orwell, who stayed in them while researching poverty in Britain.

Some of the more punitive aspects of the workhouses were missing from spikes, but the standard of housing was basic. In the 1930s there were 17,000 people in spikes in the country, and 80 were found sleeping rough during a street count in London.

It was in the 1960s that the nature of homelessness changed and public concern grew. From a post-war low of six people found sleeping rough in London in 1949, the numbers began growing. *Cathy Come Home*, the drama about homelessness, helped raise awareness of the problem. Organisations like Shelter and St Mungo's started up. St Mungo's began housing some of the hundreds sleeping rough in the capital.

By the 1980s around 20,000 single homeless people were living in accommodation for homeless people in London (now provided by charities and housing associations rather than the state). Yet, the numbers on the streets of London, for example, had risen to more than 1,000.

The reasons for this included a change in benefits stopping 16- and 17-year-olds from claiming housing benefits – with no way of paying the rent if they ran away from home, they went on the street. The closure of many of the old, crowded impersonal dormitories for homeless people and their replacement with hostels with single rooms meant that while housing standard rose, the number of beds fell. And a general increase in the number of people with drink, drug and mental health problems exacerbated the problem. Vagrancy, or to give it its modern term, rough sleeping, was on the increase again.

The government took action: though it no longer ran hostels, it set up programmes like the Rough Sleepers Initiatives and the Homeless Mentally Ill Initiative to fund extra hostels and other services. The number on the street in London fell from over 1,000 to around 600. In 1998, the present government set up the Rough Sleepers Unit to co-ordinate its approach and the efforts of the homelessness charities and the numbers on the street continue to fall.

⇨ The above information is reprinted with kind permission from St Mungo's. Visit www.mungos.org for more information.

© St Mungo's

Homelessness in Scotland

Information from the Scottish Council for Single Homelessness

Nationally how many people are homeless in Scotland?

The last fifteen years have seen a rise in homeless applications from 29,068 in 1989-90 to 59,970 in 2005-06[1]. These figures are drawn from the Scottish Executive's HL1 dataset. Every time a household presents as homeless, the local authority (LA) is required to complete a HL1 form and this is submitted electronically to the Scottish Executive. The HL1 form asks about the household's composition, the reasons for homelessness, the details of the homelessness assessment and the action which the LA has taken. The complete dataset is an invaluable source of information on homelessness in Scotland.

The most recent figures also show that over 85% of all assessed homeless applications are from both single persons and single parents. In addition to this, the 2005-06 figures reveal that single person households account for almost 80% of all households applying more than once in the period (i.e. repeat homelessness).

While more and more people are aware of their housing rights (empowered by the progressive homelessness legislation in Scotland), some people do not present as homeless to the LA as they believe they are not entitled to any help. As a result, some people may not appear in any official statistics on homelessness. This is often referred to as 'hidden homelessness', with people sleeping on friends' floors or staying with their family. Determining the level of hidden homelessness is very difficult. Some LAs have looked at their waiting lists for housing in an attempt to reveal those staying with family and friends.

Temporary accommodation

The number of households staying in temporary accommodation has risen steadily from 4,153 on 31 March 2002 to 8,135 on 31 March 2006, a

SCOTTISH COUNCIL FOR SINGLE HOMELESS

rise of 96% over the above period. The rise in the number of households in temporary accommodation is due principally to increasing numbers of homelessness applications year on year and the impact of the new duties placed on LAs under the Housing (Scotland) Act 2001 which commenced on 30 September 2002. This gave all households assessed as 'homeless and not in priority need' the right to temporary accommodation for a reasonable period of time, something they were not previously entitled too.

Rough sleepers are a small minority of homeless people but are those who are most visible

---

Households may be in temporary accommodation for a number of reasons but the majority will be waiting for permanent accommodation to let. Generally, households in temporary accommodation are finding it increasingly difficult to access suitable permanent accommodation. Indeed, many housing practitioners believe the government policy which allows tenants of LA housing to buy their house from the council ('right to buy') has led to the erosion of the LA stock available for let with many of the best homes being sold off.

LA analyses of homelessness in Scotland

Levels of homelessness vary across the country although this is partly due to differences in recording practices. The national average is approximately 12 homelessness applications per 1,000 population.

The Homelessness etc. (Scotland) Act 2003

The Housing (Scotland) Act 1987 was the first act to place specific and comprehensive duties on LAs for dealing with homelessness in their area. However, it was limited in scope. Although an applicant was found to be homeless, a number of further hurdles had to be overcome before they had an entitlement to housing.

These hurdles were 'priority need', 'intentionality' and 'local connection'. 'Priority need' was included to ensure that where supply was limited, families with children and the most vulnerable homeless people would have a right to LA accommodation. 'Intentionality' was included to counter the fear that households would give up their homes deliberately, using the homelessness route to obtain better accommodation. Finally, 'local connection' was included to prevent 'magnet' cities from being overwhelmed by homeless people from other parts of the country. The applicant's success at negotiating these hurdles determined the level of help that the LA was under a duty to provide. In effect these hurdles represented a rationing mechanism.

Currently, for those not in priority need the LA has a duty to provide advice, assistance and temporary accommodation for a reasonable period. Single homeless people usually have to have an additional need, such as a mental health problem or disability, in order to be eligible for permanent housing i.e. to give them priority need status.

The Homelessness etc. (Scotland) Act 2003 introduced a change of culture, concentrating available resources on re-housing homeless people successfully, rather than investigating whether they can be rationed out of the system. Indeed, by 2012 all unintentional homeless people will be entitled to a permanent home.

To assist LAs in providing permanent accommodation to all unintentionally homeless people the 2003 Act will phase out 'priority need' within ten years (by 2012), update the law surrounding 'intentionality' (Section 5-6: likely due date 2007) and suspend the 'local connection' provision (Section 8: due late 2006). Section 9 of the Act (which came into force in December 2004) contained a provision to enable the restriction of use of certain types of temporary accommodation for certain households. Section 11 of the Act (due to be in place by the end of 2006) places duties on private-sector landlords to inform LAs if they are evicting a tenant. Finally, the Act (through Section 12, which came into force in July 2004) enables the courts to take into account where rent arrears are the result of a delay in housing benefit payment, and therefore help to avoid unnecessary evictions.

What are the causes of homelessness?

The two most common reasons for homelessness are parents/relatives/ friends unable or unwilling to accommodate (in 2005-2006 this accounted for 36% of all detailed reasons for applying) and disputes with a partner/guardian (accounting for 22% of all detailed reasons for applying). These 'immediate' causes of homelessness may, however, disguise other underlying factors which are not recorded.

The idea that homelessness can happen to anyone is one that many people find difficult to believe. But much of the population can expect to face divorce, redundancy, mental illness etc. at some time in their lives; all of which can lead to homelessness.

A number of groups are strongly represented amongst Scotland's homeless statistics, one being people leaving institutions. In 2005-06, for example, 2,787 prison leavers found themselves without a home. SCSH believes the policy and practice of these institutions should aim to take account of the risk of homelessness after discharge and ensure that adequate support is available.

As the causes of homelessness are complex, with structural reasons such as the lack of affordable rented housing and personal reasons (as previously mentioned), SCSH believes the solutions must take this complexity into account. Homelessness is best tackled by a multi-agency approach with the individual needs of the homeless person at the centre. This could include debt counselling, action to tackle addiction, help with a rent deposit, medical treatment etc. If only one aspect of an individual's needs is addressed, it is less likely that they will be able to maintain a tenancy.

Rough sleeping

Rough sleepers are a small minority of homeless people but are those who are most visible and, more importantly, some of the most acute and complex needs. Many have experience of institutions (prison or care) and/or alcohol or drug dependency and/or mental health issues.

In 1997, the Rough Sleepers Initiative was introduced in Scotland in order to tackle rough sleeping. When the Scottish Executive took over from the Scottish Office in 1999 it set a target of ensuring that no one need sleep rough by the end of 2003 (a target which was only narrowly missed). The final evaluation of the Rough Sleepers Initiative in Scotland was published in March 2005, and Ministers have accepted the 16 recommendations contained in it. These recommendations largely focus on the need for specific targets at both a national and local level to ensure continued progress in tackling rough sleeping, and the need for robust monitoring arrangements against these targets.

The recommendations clearly pointed to a more outcomes focused approach to tackling rough sleeping. In terms of numbers of beds available, there is generally no longer any need for a person to sleep on the street, and yet people still do. There is now a need to address the reasons for this, and consider the issues that can prevent people from making use of the services available. Some of the issues which need to be considered include the quality and appropriateness of accommodation available, the knowledge of and access to such accommodation, the support needs of individuals sleeping rough and the difficulty of reaching particular sections of the rough sleeping population.

SCSH also believes that tackling rough sleeping requires concerted action by all relevant agencies including social work, health and justice services.

1 Data here relate to 'households' so the actual number of individual people affected is higher than presented
Daniel Coote, Policy Officer
20 October 2006

⇨ The above information is reprinted with kind permission from the Scottish Council for Single Homelessness. Visit www.scsh. co.uk for more information. SCSH is the national membership body for organisations and individuals working to reduce and prevent homelessness in Scotland. Our membership includes LAs, RSLs, voluntary bodies, frontline homelessness services, health and homelessness organisations, as well as a range of individual members and academics. Scottish Council for Single Homeless, Wellgate House, 200 Cowgate, Edinburgh, EH1 1NQ. Telephone: 0131 226 4382 Fax: 0131 225 4382

© Scottish Council for Single Homelessness

Homelessness myths and facts

Information from the Scottish Executive

Myth: Homeless people sleep in the street

Fact: Only a tiny proportion of homeless people are on the street. Most stay on friends' floors or with family, sometimes in precarious arrangements that can go wrong.

The legislative definition incorporates people who are living in overcrowded accommodation which is endangering their health or otherwise living in accommodation which it is unreasonable for them to occupy. There may be significant overlap between people applying under the homelessness legislation and people on waiting lists for social housing – certainly the circumstances in which people are currently living could well be very similar, yet many people would assume these groups to be entirely different.

Myth: Homeless people are antisocial or otherwise undesirable

Fact: Only a tiny proportion of homeless people have lost their accommodation because of antisocial behaviour. The vast majority have lost their accommodation because their living arrangements with family or friends have broken down, or because there's been a dispute in the household. Many people become homeless after being discharged from the armed forces or from hospital.

> Only a tiny proportion of homeless people are on the street. Most stay on friends' floors or with family, sometimes in precarious arrangements that can go wrong

Myth: People made homeless as a result of antisocial behaviour should not have any rights to social housing

Fact: All people, regardless of their actions, need housing otherwise they will have to sleep in the streets. This includes people who behave in antisocial ways. The executive is commissioning research into the best ways of breaking the cycle of antisocial behaviour. Existing projects – such as Dundee Families Project – aimed at helping families with antisocial behaviour can be very effective.

Myth: Homeless people should be allocated any accommodation available and should be grateful for it

Fact: If homeless people are allocated poor quality accommodation then they are more likely to become homeless again as they feel vulnerable and unsupported. No one should have to live in poor quality accommodation in Scotland in the 21st century and this is why the Scottish government and the housing agency Communities Scotland are working with local authorities to ensure that housing meets acceptable quality levels.

⇨ The above information is reprinted with kind permission from the Scottish Executive. Visit www.scotland.gov.uk for more information.
© *Scottish Executive*

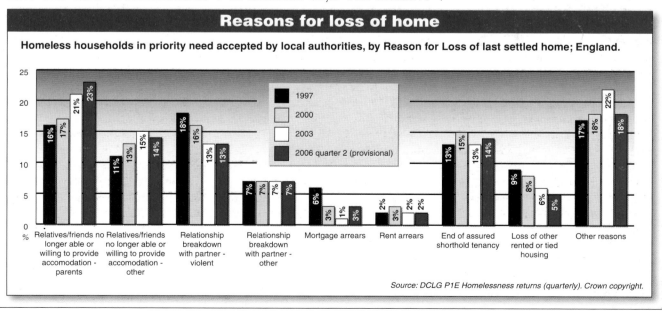

Reasons for loss of home

Homeless households in priority need accepted by local authorities, by Reason for Loss of last settled home; England.

Legend: 1997, 2000, 2003, 2006 quarter 2 (provisional)

Reason	1997	2000	2003	2006 q2
Relatives/friends no longer able or willing to provide accomodation - parents	16%	17%	21%	23%
Relatives/friends no longer able or willing to provide accomodation - other	11%	13%	15%	14%
Relationship breakdown with partner - violent	18%	16%	13%	13%
Relationship breakdown with partner - other	7%	7%	7%	7%
Mortgage arrears	6%	3%	1%	3%
Rent arrears	2%	3%	2%	2%
End of assured shorthold tenancy	13%	15%	13%	14%
Loss of other rented or tied housing	9%	8%	6%	5%
Other reasons	17%	18%	22%	18%

Source: DCLG P1E Homelessness returns (quarterly). Crown copyright.

Housing and homelessness

What's the real problem?

It doesn't sound like too much to ask, does it?

Good housing for everyone. We're not talking mansions, just a decent place to live, a home from which to face the world.

In a civilised society like ours, everyone should have access to a proper home – and we all know that a home is much more than just a physical shelter. How we are housed affects our health, education, freedom, dignity, security, family life and the communities we live in. So why are people still enduring the misery of sleeping rough or raising children in squalor?

The reasons are complex but one thing is sure – there is a desperate shortage of good, affordable housing in the UK. All of us should be concerned about this. All of us can help in some way.

Homelessness and the threat of homelessness remain a daily reality for many families, couples and single people. Poor housing conditions affect many more throughout the length and breadth of the country. The lack of a decent home threatens every area of a person's life – employment, health, relationships and education.

Christian vision in action **HOUSING JUSTICE**

Some of the key issues in housing and homelessness

There is a severe shortage of private rented accommodation accessible to those on a low income. The shortage is most acute in London and the South East where many workers are on low wages and rents are high. Many potential tenants cannot afford a deposit or rent in advance while most private landlords will not accept tenants receiving housing benefit. People under 25 are particularly disadvantaged by the single room rent regulations.

House prices are at a historic high pushing buying a house out of reach of all but the richest in society. Today an average house costs over £158,00 whilst the average income is around £26,000 – houses thus cost more than six times the average income. The average figure masks large variations across the country – prices are highest in London where on average over £205,000 is needed to buy a house. Figures from the Halifax show that housing is affordable to first-time buyers in 92% of places in the UK.

> **In a civilised society like ours, everyone should have access to a proper home – and we all know that a home is much more than just a physical shelter**

Social house building is at low levels – last year only 20,000 new housing association homes and virtually no council homes were built. Since 1979 over 1.6million council houses have been sold under the right-to-buy policy – these have not been replaced. A government expert in 2004 estimated that we need to be building at least another 23,000 new social homes a year to meet ongoing demand and begin to address the backlog.

The number of people applying as homeless is at an all-time high. In the year April 2004 – March 2005, 266,870 decisions on homelessness applications were made by local authorities in England. (Statistical release 14 March 2005: Statutory Homelessness: 1st Quarter 2005, ENGLAND from the Office of the Deputy Prime Minister [ODPM].)

There are marked regional variations in the number of acceptances of homelessness. London accounts for a fifth of England's homelessness acceptances but areas such as the North East and Yorkshire and Humberside where there is a plentiful supply of housing still have higher than average numbers of homelessness acceptances.

In the third quarter of 2005 there were over 101,000 families in temporary accommodation which is often unsuitable, insecure and expensive. Some of it is private rented housing, some is shared hostels and bed and breakfast hotels and some is hard-to-let council stock. Living in temporary accommodation is hard for families and children in particular are affected as their schooling and home life is disrupted which can put them at a disadvantage for the rest of their lives.

Proving eligibility for re-housing under the homelessness legislation can be difficult, especially if the person has to demonstrate vulnerability.

Homelessness is caused by many factors, often beyond a person's control, such as the ending of a private tenancy, unemployment, bereavement, relationship breakdown, debt, ill health. The most common reason for homelessness (38% of cases) arises because parents, relatives or friends (mostly parents) are no longer willing or able to provide accommodation.

Many tenants, both social and private, live in substandard accommodation which threatens their health. They have little bargaining power to get the landlord to carry out the repairs, or opportunities for a transfer to another more suitable property.

Single people and childless couples including young people are still largely excluded from access to local authority housing.

The administration of Housing Benefit (a means-tested benefit to contribute towards the cost of rents) is slow and often inaccurate, resulting in claimants being threatened with homelessness and even made homeless due to non-payment of rent. The level of housing benefit is restricted, which affects a claimant's ability to find a property in the private sector in areas of high demand and high rent levels.

The complexities of the law, the lack of housing options and the causes of homelessness all contribute to threaten the lives of those in society least able to look after themselves.

⇨ The above information is reprinted with kind permission from Housing Justice. Visit www.justhousing.org.uk for more information.

© Housing Justice

Street homelessness

Information from Shelter

Homelessness has a broad meaning; it can be used for people living in homes that are unsuitable, as well as for people who are sleeping rough. The Government has achieved its target of reducing the number of people sleeping rough by two-thirds. In many parts of the country there are outreach teams to help those on the streets, hostels providing the first step off the streets, as well as day centres and other agencies offering training and support to access employment and cultural projects. However, still too many people are not receiving the help they need, at the time they need it, and end up sleeping rough on the streets.

This article looks at how many people are sleeping rough; some of the main factors which make it more likely that somebody may end up sleeping on the streets; the crossover between homelessness and other street lifestyles; access to accommodation and support; government policies on rough sleeping and Shelter's own prevention work.

What is street homelessness?

Homelessness means not having a home. A home is a place that provides security, and links to a community and support network. It needs to be decent and affordable.

Under the law, even if someone has a roof over their head they can still be homeless. This is because they may not have the right to stay where they live or their home may be unsuitable to live in.

Rough sleeping is defined by the Government as 'people sleeping, or bedded down, in the open air (such as on the streets, or in doorways, parks or bus shelters); people in buildings or other places not designed for habitation (such as barns, sheds, car parks, cars, derelict boats, stations, or "bashes")'.

Street homelessness is a much wider term than rough sleeping, taking into account the street lifestyles of some people who may not actually sleep on the streets. Street homeless people are those who routinely find themselves on the streets during the day with nowhere to go at night. Some will end up sleeping outside, or in a derelict or other building not designed for human habitation, perhaps for long periods. Others will sleep at a friend's for a very short time, or stay in a hostel, night-shelter or squat, or spend nights in prison or hospital.

Although this article explores many aspects of street homelessness from rough sleeping to street drinking and begging, it is important to be aware that much of the research referred to focuses specifically on rough sleepers.

How many people are street homeless?

Government figures

The Government uses the results of street counts, undertaken by local authorities and voluntary agencies, to estimate the number of people 'sleeping rough' on a single night. To be included in a count a person must be 'bedded down', e.g. sleeping in a place covered by street counts.

It is widely recognised that the counts do not reflect the full extent of rough sleeping. Count staff may not locate rough sleepers who have hidden themselves in disused buildings or stayed in areas away from those covered by the count. To avoid any double counting, people who are not actually sleeping at the time of the count are not included in the figures, even if it is likely that they will go on to spend the night sleeping rough.

The latest government figures estimate that there are 459 people sleeping rough on any given night in England. Of these, nearly 50 per cent sleep rough in London. A report for the Office of the Deputy Prime Minister, however, has acknowledged that the number of people sleeping rough over the course of a year is at least ten times higher than the snapshot on any given night provided by the street counts.

Despite this, results from street counts do provide useful information about the relative extent of rough sleeping in different areas and also allow some analysis of trends in rough sleeping over time. According to figures from street counts, the number of people sleeping rough on any given night since 1998 has decreased by more than a third.

Other figures
Combined Homelessness and Information Network
The Combined Homelessness and Information Network (CHAIN), is a database used by agencies working with street homeless people in London. CHAIN figures show that during 2004/05 a total of 3,112 people were contacted on the streets of London by outreach teams. Of these, 45 per cent (1,400) were 'new contacts' eg people who had not been contacted on the street in previous years.

Shelter
During 2005, Shelter services in England worked with 4,000 single men, women and couples without children who were street homeless.

Demographic profile of street homeless people
Gender
Around 90 per cent of those sleeping rough are men. During 2004/05 the outreach teams in London contacted 3,112 people. Of these, 89 per cent were men (2,756) and the remaining 11 per cent were women (356).
Age
A large proportion of people sleeping rough are between 26 and 49 years old. For example, in London 73 per cent of those contacted by outreach teams during 2004/5 were between these ages. Eighteen per cent were aged 50 or over and 10 per cent were aged under 25.

Street homelessness is a much wider term than rough sleeping, taking into account the street lifestyles of some people who may not actually sleep on the streets

---

Ethnicity
Most surveys estimate that about 90 per cent of people sleeping on the streets are white, including significant minorities of white Irish and Scottish people. However, there is evidence that the profile of rough sleepers is becoming increasingly diverse.

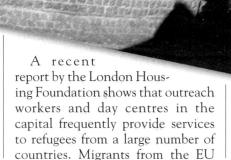

A recent report by the London Housing Foundation shows that outreach workers and day centres in the capital frequently provide services to refugees from a large number of countries. Migrants from the EU accession states are also present in the rough sleeping population. A survey of London winter shelters in 2004 found that there was a total of 30 different nationalities represented amongst those staying in the shelters.

Why do people become street homeless?
Although the reasons for becoming homeless differ between each person, there are common factors. Some are personal; related to the family, community and individual, and others are structural; relating to the economy, the law, social trends, and the national housing system. Homelessness is likely to be caused by a combination of structural and personal factors. There are, however, risk factors which make it more likely that a person could become street homeless. These include:
⇨ family conflict and/or relationship breakdown between partners
⇨ leaving institutions
⇨ mental health problems
⇨ substance misuse
⇨ dual diagnosis (mental health problem/s combined with substance misuse)
⇨ financial problems
⇨ having 'no recourse to public funds' (e.g. no social security)
⇨ refugees or people seeking asylum.

It is important to note that while the above are risk factors, most people who experience these problems do not become street homeless.
Family conflict and/or relationship breakdown between partners
Family conflict and relationship breakdown can lead to street homelessness when people have to, or are asked to leave their home.

Family conflict: A high proportion of people who sleep rough have a history of family conflict. One study found that 21 per cent of homeless people gave this as the main reason for sleeping rough, rising to 37 per cent of people aged under 26. Furthermore, 33 per cent of homeless people gave this as one of their reasons for first sleeping rough.

Relationship breakdown between partners: A survey among people who had slept rough found that 45 per cent of them reported experience of relationship breakdown. Twenty-five per cent of these slept rough straight away after the relationship broke down.

Leaving institutions

People leaving institutions can lack support networks from families or communities that may have helped them find accommodation, or prevented them from becoming street homeless.

Local authority care

Surveys carried out among people sleeping rough found that between a quarter and a third have spent time in local authority care. Care leavers sometimes face difficulties both finding somewhere to live and accessing the support needed to live independently. Care leavers often do not have the financial and practical support offered by the family. A small-scale survey in 2001 found that still about a quarter of rough sleepers had spent time in local authority care, however, these were older rough sleepers who had spent time in local authority care as children, not generally young people who had just left care.

Leaving prison or young offenders' institutions

Around half of people sleeping rough have either been in prison or to a young offenders' institution, and many have had repeated contact with the police and courts. A survey among people sleeping rough in 2001 found that two-thirds (64 per cent) had served a custodial sentence.

People leaving prison often have nowhere to live on their release. Difficulties finding employment can make it harder to pay for accommodation. It is common for people to lose accommodation whilst they are in prison if they are unable to keep up rent or mortgage payments.

Armed forces

Major research in 1997 showed that 25 per cent of people sleeping rough on the streets of London had served in the armed forces. Another survey in 2001 showed that only 14 per cent of rough sleepers had served in the armed forces. This may suggest that older rough sleepers have been moved

off the streets, although the figure still remains relatively high. There are a number of reasons suggested for this, including lack of experience living independently; housekeeping and budgeting; spending years living an institutionalised life; the late entry into the housing market; a culture of heavy drinking while in the forces; and a lack of community ties.

Mental health problems

The links between homelessness and mental health are complex; it can be a cause or a consequence of homelessness. Research undertaken in 1996 found that 60 per cent of people sleeping rough may have had mental health problems. Another survey found that 30 per cent of rough sleepers had a current diagnosed psychotic illness, and people who had slept rough for a year or more were more likely to have had multiple psychiatric admissions. For people sleeping on the streets it is very difficult to gain and sustain access to psychiatric and social services, which results in further deterioration of their mental health.

Substance misuse

People with substance misuse problems can sometimes lose their homes due to rent or mortgage arrears, others may find the practical aspects of managing a tenancy difficult and 'abandon' their homes. Substance misuse can also lead to family disputes and time spent in prison.

Research has also found that in some cases homelessness itself can

trigger the commencement of, or an escalation in, drug use. About 20 per cent of young street homeless people reported in a survey that they started to use drugs after they became homeless, predominantly because it was the first time they were exposed to drugs. Other street homeless people use drugs as a coping strategy for dealing with the difficulties of homelessness. Fifty per cent of street homeless people taking part in research conducted by Crisis cited drug use as a reason for becoming homeless, and 36 per cent cited the use of alcohol as a reason. During 2004/05, 35 per cent of people contacted by outreach teams in London had a drug problem and 32 per cent had alcohol problems. 'Dual diagnosis' is the term for the combination of mental health and alcohol and/or drug problems. The outreach teams in London recorded that 23 per cent of rough sleepers have a dual diagnosis.

Financial problems

Rent or mortgage arrears, or the loss of income due to unemployment or illness, are both common reasons why people lose their homes. In some cases, these kinds of financial problems can lead to street homelessness. In a study of rough sleepers, 26 per cent of those interviewed stated that arrears or other money problems were a reason for sleeping rough.

Refugees and asylum seekers

Recent research found that refugees and asylum seekers are overrepresented in the street homeless population. In Leicester alone, over a five-week period in 2006, 308 refugees and asylum seekers approached agencies participating in the research reporting they were destitute. Of these, one-third reported sleeping rough in locations such as underpasses, the train station and the market. The other two-thirds reported sleeping on friends' floors.

The main reason found behind the destitution of asylum seekers was, following a failed asylum claim, a reluctance to sign up for voluntary return to countries they considered unsafe. For refugees, one reason behind destitution is the requirement for individuals who are granted asylum to leave the accommodation provided by National Asylum Support Service (NASS) within 28 days. New refugees may find it hard to access housing advice to help them find accommodation, as the time allowed is often not long enough. There is evidence that these factors can result in street homelessness for new refugees, especially single men who are not eligible for emergency accommodation from the local authority.

This research also found that many street homeless refugees had been long-term residents in the UK before they became homeless. Reasons for this might include problems integrating into a new culture and language barriers, which can result in difficulty accessing employment, education and other services. In some cases, there may be issues relating to the experiences which led the individual to seek asylum, which may affect their ability to find and keep a home, for example, suffering Post Traumatic Stress Syndrome.

Having 'no recourse to public funds'

Foreign nationals who don't have recourse to public funds are sometimes ineligible for services available to other rough sleepers. This exacerbates their problems by making it harder for them to move off the streets.

People arriving from EU accession states are not entitled to housing benefit until they have been working continuously in the UK for a year. This means they sometimes sleep

---

Around 90 per cent of rough sleepers are men

rough before they are able to secure employment and therefore money for accommodation and, after a period of time, the right to welfare benefits.

Failed asylum seekers who are moved out of NASS accommodation while they wait for a safe passage home are another group represented in the street population without recourse to public funds. This group is not legally allowed to work in the UK and so cannot seek employment as a means to securing money for accommodation.

Those with no recourse to public funds cannot access hostels for single homeless people, although there are some night shelters and day centres for street homeless people they can use.

⇨ The above information is an extract from the Shelter factsheet *Street Homelessness* and is reprinted with permission. To view the full document or for more information, visit www.shelter.org.uk

© Shelter 2006

Street lifestyles

Information from Shelter

There is a lack of clarity about the relationship and crossover between rough sleepers and other people who participate in the following street-based activities, but who have accommodation. A street lifestyle can precede, accompany or follow periods of street homelessness, or be maintained while a person has long-term accommodation. Street lifestyles can also encourage rough sleeping and provide a route into sleeping on the streets. Agencies who traditionally work with rough sleepers are increasingly expanding their services to reach people who are in accommodation but living a street lifestyle.

Street drinking

Alcohol Concern's definition of a street drinker is 'a person who drinks very heavily in public and, at least in the short term, is unable or unwilling to control his or her drinking'. Many street drinkers consume alcohol in groups known as drinking schools, which are a source of companionship for members. A survey among people who beg and/or drink found that of all those surveyed, over half had slept rough the previous night. People who beg were more likely (67 per cent) than people who drink (21 per cent) to sleep rough.

Begging

Although begging and homelessness are inextricably linked, not all rough sleepers beg or vice versa. However, the vast majority of those who beg are in unstable accommodation. Research found that only six individuals, out of a sample of 260 people who beg, were living in their own home.

Sex work

Another group that overlaps with the street population are people who are engaged in street-based sex work. Research has found that female sex workers form one of the most excluded and marginalised groups of homeless people. These women often sleep in cars, parks, crack houses, on friends' floors and sometimes on the streets, but are generally not engaged in programmes set up to assist street homeless people.

⇨ The above information is an extract from *Street Homelessness*, published by Shelter, and is reprinted with permission. Visit www.shelter.org.uk for more information or to view the full document.

© Shelter 2006

Statistics about homelessness

Information from Crisis

Fighting for hope for homeless people

Numbers

Rough sleepers

⇨ Government street counts estimate there are about 502 people sleeping outside around England on any one night, compared with nearly 2,000 (1,850) in 1998. Representing a fall of 73%. 289 of these are in Greater London (against 508 and 265 respectively in June 2004) (ODPM, July 2005).

⇨ Outside London, the largest concentrations of rough sleepers in England are found in Reading (11), Sheffield (10), Brighton and Hove (9), Exeter (8), Liverpool (8) and Northampton (8) (ODPM, July 2005).

⇨ Broadway report that 2,807 people slept rough in London alone, during 2005/06 (Broadway Street to Home, 2006).

Statutory homeless households in England

⇨ In 2005, local authorities accepted 100,170 households (not individuals) as unintentionally homeless and in priority need (compared to just over 100,000 1997), and were therefore owed the main duty to be housed by the local authority. This number was down from the 127,760 households accepted in 2004.

⇨ However a much larger number of households, 162,990, were actually found to be homeless by local authorities in 2005.

⇨ In 2005 only 47,800 single homeless households were categorised as in priority need and therefore found some form of accommodation by the local authority compared to 48,990 not in priority need. Therefore single homeless households that do apply for support are more likely to be categorised as 'homeless and not in priority need' and therefore not owed a duty by the local authority to be found some form of accommodation.

⇨ In addition 13,830 households were considered intentionally homeless and in priority need. This is a higher number than every year since 1997 when 4,960 households were found to be intentionally homeless and a higher percentage of all applications made at 6%.

⇨ In London 22,700 households were accepted in 2005 by their local authorities as being homeless and in priority need, and 35,050 households were registered as homeless.

Statutory homeless households in Scotland

⇨ In the period 2004/2005, local authorities accepted 29,546 households as homeless and priority need. This was 74% of the households who were assessed as homeless [39,681].

⇨ 17,278 of priority need households were single homeless households without children [single people without children or couples without children] compared to 9,950 non-priority single homeless households.

⇨ The last fourteen years have seen a rise in homeless applications from 29,068 in 1989-90 to 54,829 in 2003-04.

⇨ Results from the 2001-2002 Scottish Household survey suggest that one in every five homeless households do not apply to their local authority.

Hidden homeless people

⇨ There are around 380,000 single homeless people in Great Britain. This includes those staying in hostels, B&Bs, squats, on friends' floors and in overcrowded accommodation (Crisis, *How Many, How Much?*, 2003).

Placed in temporary accommodation

⇨ In the period July to September 2004 the numbers of households housed in temporary accommodation by local authorities first exceeded 100,000. Since then the numbers have

remained excess of 100,000 until the final quarter of 2005 when the numbers in temporary accommodation reduced to 98,730 (ODPM, *Homelessness Statistics*, 2005).

⇨ Over recent years the percentage of households who spend 2 or more years in temporary accommodation or recorded as homeless at home has been increasing. In the fourth quarter of 2005, 33% of households in London had previously spent 2 or more years in temporary accommodation or homeless at home, four times as high as the same period in 2000 and 6% higher than first quarter of 2005 (ODPM, *Homelessness Statistics*, 2005).

⇨ Overall there has been a steady decrease in the numbers of households being housed in B&Bs from a high of 13,950 in the third quarter of 2002, to 4,950 in December 2005 (ODPM, *Homelessness Statistics*, 2005).

⇨ London had the highest number of households in temporary accommodation on 31 December, accounting for 65 per cent of the England total. It was also the only region to show an increase in the numbers in temporary accommodation by 1% to 63,800 households

⇨ In Scotland as at 31 March 2005 there were 7,539 households in temporary accommodation arranged by local authorities. This has risen steadily from 4,420 on 30 June 2002. 2,373 households were with dependent children.

Becoming homeless
⇨ The average time between the triggers that lead to homelessness and when homelessness finally occurs is nine years (Centre for the Analysis of Social Exclusion, *Routes into Homelessness*, 2000)

⇨ The four-week rule is the process by which newly homeless people become acclimatised to life on the street. After that they become entrenched and it becomes more difficult for them to move back into mainstream society (Crisis, *Homelessness Factfile*, 1998).

Profile and background
Age
⇨ Around 25 per cent of rough sleepers are aged between 18 and 25, and six per cent are over 60 (SEU, July 1998).

⇨ An age breakdown of those accepted as statutorily homeless is not available from English local authority statistics but in Scotland the majority (60%) of the homeless households without dependent children were aged 25 or over and it is this age group where most of the increases

---

Government street counts estimate there are about 502 people sleeping outside around England on any one night, compared with nearly 2,000 (1,850) in 1998

---

in homelessness have been happening (Scottish Executive, *Statistical Bulletin*).

Gender
⇨ Around 80 to 90 per cent of rough sleepers are male (SEU, July 1998; Scottish Executive *Rough Sleepers Initiative* 2004; Crisis, *Homelessness Factfile* 2003).

⇨ Numbers of single homeless women has risen significantly in recent years (Fitzpatrick 2000).

⇨ There are also a growing number of homeless women on the streets and in emergency night shelters and hostels across Britain (May, Cloke and Johnsen 2004).

Ethnic origin
⇨ BME groups are more likely to sleep on friends' and family's floors (Crisis, *Homelessness Factfile*, 2003).

⇨ Only a quarter of young black Africans and a third of young Afro-Caribbeans reported sleeping rough in 1997/8 – compared to over half of young white people (Centrepoint, *Hidden Statistics*, 2000).

⇨ Black and minority ethnic households represent 21 per cent of those accepted by local authorities as homeless in England, but only eight per cent of the general population of England (ODPM, 2005).

⇨ In 2005 100,170 households were accepted as homeless and in priority need in England. Their ethnic origin was as follows:
  ↳ 74,460 White [74.3%]
  ↳ 10,330 African Caribbean [10.3%]
  ↳ 5,290 Pakistani/Bangladeshi [5.3%]
  ↳ 5,110 other ethnic origin [5.1%]
  ↳ 4,970 ethnic origin not known [5%].

Local authority care
⇨ Between 18% to 32% of rough sleepers were once in local authority care as children (Randall and Brown 2001, CHAIN London 2001/02). This compares to national figures which show that only one per cent of all those under 18 have been in care (SEU, July 1998).

Young people
⇨ Between 36,000 to 52,000 young people are estimated to have been 'found homeless' by local authorities in England in 2003 (Centrepoint Youth Homelessness Index, 2004).

⇨ It can be estimated that 1 in 8 of those homeless young people (up to 6,700) may have recent experience of rough sleeping (Centrepoint).

- In 2004 9% (10,930) of those accepted as statutory homeless and in priority need by local authorities in England was due to them being a 'Young Person' (ODPM 2005).
- It is likely that several thousand young people experience homelessness without having any contact with local authorities in England each year (Centrepoint).

Young people who become homeless are more likely to have lived with stepparents, foster parents or relatives by the age of 12 than those who do not become homeless

- Family conflict is the main immediate cause of homelessness amongst at least two-thirds of homeless young people (Crisis, *Trouble at Home*, 2001).
- 86 per cent of young homeless people are forced to leave home rather than choose to (SEU, July 1998).
- Two-thirds of young homeless people leave school with no qualifications (Mental Health Foundation, *Off to a Bad Start*, 1996).
- Young people who become homeless are more likely to have lived with stepparents, foster parents or relatives by the age of 12 than those who do not become homeless (Safe in the City, *Taking Risks*, 1999).
- 45 per cent of young homeless people have experienced violence in the family home on more than one occasion (Safe in the City, *Taking Risks*, 1999).
- One-third of young homeless people have attempted suicide – a fifth within the past year (Craig T. et al, *Off to a Bad Start*, 1996).

Prison
- Around half of rough sleepers have been in prison or a remand centre at some time (SEU, July 1998).

- Around one-third of prisoners who are about to be released report having nowhere to stay. Around 28,500 people are homeless on leaving prison each year (SEU, 2002).

Women
- Around 10 to 25% of single homeless people on the streets and in hostels are women. The proportion of women among young single homeless people is however higher – 20 to 40% (Crisis Homelessness Factfile Online, 2003).
- 63 per cent of women aged 30-49 cite domestic violence as the key reason for their homelessness (Crisis, *Out of Sight, Out of Mind? – The Experience of Homeless Women*, 1999).
- In 2004 5% (6,160) of those accepted as statutory homeless and in priority need by local authorities in England was due to domestic violence (ODPM, 2005).
- 1 in 4 women experience domestic violence over their lifetimes and between 6-10% of women suffer domestic violence in a given year (Council of Europe, 2002).
- 40 per cent of young women who become homeless have experienced sexual abuse in childhood or adolescence (SEU, 1998).

- Homeless women are twice as likely as men to have lived with foster parents (Anderson, Kemp and Quilgars, *Single Homeless People*, 1993)
- One in four young female hostel residents are pregnant in any given year (Crisis, *Homeless Young Women and Pregnancy*, 2000)
- The low profile of women in homelessness statistics can probably be accounted for by

the fact that women – and people from ethnic minorities – make better use of their social networks than white males to find alternative solutions to their housing problems (such as staying with family or friends) (Crisis, *Out of Sight, Out of Mind?* 1999).

Relationship breakdown
- In England in 2004 38% households are homeless because relatives or friends are no longer willing to provide accommodation – the percentage has been slowly increasing over the years (ODPM, 2005).
- Another 20% of households are homeless due to the breakdown of the relationship (13% is due to domestic violence) (ODPM, 2005).
- Around one in four hostel residents left their last permanent home because of family or relationship breakdown (Crisis, *Trouble at Home*, 2001).
- Surveys routinely show that around half of homeless people ascribe their homelessness to relationship breakdown (Crisis, *A Future Foretold*, 1999).

Education and employment
- A recent St Mungo's survey identified that 5% of London's homeless are currently in some form of employment but that this proportion has decreased from 86% in 1986 (St Mungo's, 2005).
- Of the *Big Issue* vendors in northern England, 79% had been employed (The Big Issue in the North, 2000).
- A Crisis survey of 150 homeless people across the UK found that 47% possess qualifications; of those 48% have GCSEs, 16% have A levels, 15% have a degree and 13% have professional qualifications (Crisis, 2002).

March 2006

- Crisis is the national charity for single homeless people. Its mission is to fight homelessness and empower people to fulfil their potential and transform their lives. For more information, please visit the Crisis website at www.crisis.org.uk

© Crisis

23-year low in new cases of homelessness

Information from the Department for Communities and Local Government

New cases of homelessness have fallen to levels not seen since the early 1980s, Housing Minister Yvette Cooper announced today.

National statistics released today show that just under 19,500 new households became homeless during April to June of this year. This is nearly 30% lower than the same time last year (the biggest such percentage reduction ever recorded) and continues the downward trend seen since the beginning of 2004.

The figures also show a continued reduction of households in temporary accommodation, down 7% compared to the same time last year. There has been a steady drop in the number of households in temporary accommodation over the last six months – the figure having now reduced to 93,910.

Yvette Cooper also announced today that the Prime Minister's target, to reduce rough sleeping numbers by two-thirds, is being sustained. Today's statistics show that there are around 500 rough sleepers in England on any given night.

Welcoming the news the Housing Minister said:

'We've made great progress in preventing and tackling homelessness with numbers falling to a twenty three year low. This record reduction shows the success of prevention schemes funded by £300m worth of government investment. Rough sleeping has also dropped by more than two-thirds since 1998.

Statistics show that there are around 500 rough sleepers in England on any given night

---

'As we approach the 40th anniversary of *Cathy Come Home*, this government has introduced a safety net which is amongst the strongest in the world and provides protection for families with children like Cathy.

'However, there are still too many people in temporary accommodation and overcrowded conditions and we need to continue the work to prevent rough sleeping. The challenge is to provide more settled homes. That's why we need to build more homes across the board – more market housing, more social housing, more homes for shared equity and more affordable homes.'

Since 2003 Local Authorities have had strategies in place to prevent and tackle homelessness.

By 2008 the Government will have invested £300m for prevention services; schemes include rent deposit schemes and mediation services.

The Government has committed to increasing the rate of house building to 200,000 new homes each year by 2016 to address the supply and affordability problems. We also plan to build an extra 10,000 social homes a year by 2008 – a 50 per cent increase on current rates. The government is also consulting on raising the overcrowding standard, and have invested £20m to help tackle the problem.

The Government is committed to reducing the number of households in temporary accommodation by 50 per cent by 2010. While 85 per cent of households in temporary accommodation are living in self-contained housing, they do not provide the security and opportunities a settled home brings.
11 September 2006

⇨ The above information is reprinted with kind permission from the Department for Communities and Local Government. For more information on this and other issues, please visit the DCLG department's website at www.communities.gov.uk

Older homelessness

Facts and figures

The low priority given to older homeless people is reflected in the lack of comprehensive statistical evidence showing the true extent of the problem. The following figures give an indication of older homelessness based on the most recent research available. Older homeless people are defined by the UK Coalition on Older Homelessness as those who are 50+ and are sleeping rough or living in inappropriate temporary accommodation, or are at risk of imminent homelessness.

Why are older homeless people less visible than other groups?

The vast majority of older homeless people are invisible because they are often trapped in unsuitable temporary accommodation. Older people sleeping rough frequently hide from view and are not easily identifiable. One study found that 70% of those sleeping rough stayed in isolated or hidden spots (Crane 1997). Older homeless people may not have any contact with statutory or voluntary services, so their needs are not registered. They may not be in receipt of any benefits and will not appear in official housing statistics if they have referred themselves to a bed and breakfast hotel. Official

Frontline agencies in partnership

statistics only show those older people accepted by local authorities as vulnerably homeless due to age and this is dependent on the interpretation of the homelessness legislation adopted by individual local authorities (Crane 1997).

Older people sleeping rough

How many older people are sleeping rough?
In 2003 2,808 people were contacted on the streets by outreach teams in London. 18% of them (527 people) were over the age of 50 (CHAIN 2004). There are lots of problems with the rough sleeper counts, particularly for this population who are more likely to be hidden. Across England the official figures from the rough sleeper counts and HIP returns from local authorities for June 2004 are that there were 508 people sleeping rough in England on any single night (ODPM 2004). In Scotland the figure for 2003 was 328 people (Scottish Executive 2003).

There are no official figures for Wales but estimates are in the hundreds. The evidence is that between 18 and 39% of rough sleepers are over the age of 50 years (CHAIN and Crane 1999).
Are older people more vulnerable on the streets?
St Mungo's have recently carried out a survey of 1,534 homeless people on the streets and in emergency shelters. They found that 1 in 4 are over 50 years of age. 50% of those people had been homeless for over 2 years. The survey looked at the multiple problems experienced by older homeless people on top of homelessness. 56% are alcohol dependent, 48% have mental health problems, 47% have physical health problems, 25% have challenging behaviour issues. Many of these problems overlap, 43% of the older people surveyed had 4 or more problems in addition to their homelessness (St Mungo's 2004). This is consistent with findings from research with homeless link member agencies on working with people with multiple needs which showed that almost 60% of people they were working with over the age of 50 had three or more presenting problems in addition to homelessness (Bevan and Van Doorn 2002). Many older people do not survive sleeping rough over an extended period and die without any recognition of their plight or circumstances. Studies in the 1990s for Crisis found that the average age of death of people recorded as homeless on coroners' reports varies between 42 and 53 years of age (Grenier 1996, Keyes and Kennedy 1992). Because of the effects of rough sleeping on physical and mental health the ageing process is often accelerated. This means that even people in their 50s may exhibit health problems normally associated with an older population. Older people sleeping rough are in greater danger on the streets and are more likely to be physically assaulted

(Grenier 1996). Some older people avoid using day centres or hostels due to a fear that they may be assaulted or robbed.

Older people in temporary accommodation

How many older people are living in hostels?

An estimated 5,000 older people are living in inappropriate hostel accommodation in England. This figure has been reached using CORE data of people in supported housing on a temporary basis. This does not include smaller providers, but does include some types of supported housing that are not hostel like (Pannell and Palmer 2004). Recent research by Homeless Link shows that hostel beds in London are silted up with 46% of people ready to move on but unable to for lack of options. People are waiting between 12 and 18 months in hostels after they are ready, the waiting time is longer for those needing supported accommodation.

How many older people are living in bed and breakfast hotels?

It is estimated that there are 12,000 older people self placed in Bed and Breakfasts or other boarded accommodation at any one time in the UK. This estimate is derived from DWP information on those in receipt of Housing Benefit. Around 6,000 are aged 50-64 and 6,000 aged 65+. There is no information about the average length of stay and so no basis for estimating an over-the-year figure (Pannell and Palmer 2004).

Other groups of homeless people

It is estimated that there are 24,000 older people staying with friends or family in overcrowded conditions in England. They are not the owner or tenant of the property (nor their partner) and at least one adult does not have their own bedroom. The accommodation is insecure because such people have no legally enforceable right to stay there. It is also inadequate because the older person or one of the other adults has to sleep in the living room or share inappropriately. It is estimated there are, at any one point in time, 500 older people at imminent risk of eviction and 100 older people due to be released from prison with

nowhere to go. The number of older people due for discharge from hospital with no appropriate home to go to is unknown (Pannell and Palmer 2004).

Conclusions

How many older people are unofficially homeless in England and Wales?

Based on the statistical information outlined above we can roughly estimate that up to 42,000 older people are unofficially homeless in England and Wales (Pannell and Palmer).

How many older people homeless people are 'officially' accepted as homeless by their local authority?

In the year to April 2003, 4,420 households were accepted as statutorily homeless in England because of vulnerability related to old age. This represented 3% of all acceptances in England (ODPM 2004). However, guidance to local authorities suggests that 'old age' should be defined as people aged 60+, although some local authorities may consider people aged 50+. This means that most older people over 50 may not be accepted as homeless due to old age depending on the interpretation of individual local authorities (Crane 1999).

Are politicians aware of problems facing older homeless people?

There is a lack of awareness of older homelessness as a specific aspect of the overall problem. An analysis of *Hansard* showed that between October 1998 and July 2000, there

were 326 items on homelessness, of which 24% referred to young people, yet less than one per cent made any reference at all to older people (Warnes and Crane 2000).

Sources

⇨ Bevan, P. and van Doorn, A. 2002. *Good Practice Briefing on Multiple Needs*. Homeless Link.

---

1 in 4 homeless people are over 50 years of age. 50% of those people had been homeless for over 2 years

---

⇨ CHAIN Annual Rough Sleeping Bulletin for London Broadway 2003.
⇨ Crane, M. 1999. *Understanding Older Homeless People*. Open University Press.
⇨ Warnes, T & Crane, M. 2000. Unpublished research study commissioned by: Bondway HA, St Mungo's, and Thames Reach.
⇨ Crane, M. 1997. *Homeless Truths: Challenging the Myths about Older Homeless People*. Help the Aged
⇨ Grenier, P. 1996. *Still Dying for a Home*. Crisis
⇨ Keyes, S. and Kennedy, M. 1992. *Sick to death of homelessness. An Investigation into the links between homelessness, health and Mortality*. Crisis.
⇨ ODPM Homelessness statistics 2003/2004.
⇨ Pannell, J. and Palmer, G. 2004. *Coming of Age: opportunities for older homeless people under Supporting People*. Coalition on Older Homelessness.
⇨ St Mungo's. *The Big Survey 50-50*. November 2004.

⇨ The above information is reprinted with kind permission from the UK Coalition on Older Homelessness, a project of Homeless Link. Visit www. olderhomelessness.org.uk for more information.

Asylum and immigration

Information from Homeless Link

Migrants, refugees and asylum seekers can be especially vulnerable to homelessness. They may lack the support networks of friends and family able to offer them a place to stay in a crisis. New arrivals may also have difficulties with language and understanding the British system, which can make it harder to access support services. There are sometimes uncertainties and limitations around entitlement to state benefit and support. This in turn may limit access to help such as hostel accommodation.

The issues

People come to the UK for a variety of reasons; to study, work and live under a number of different schemes and legislation. Their positions vary depending on where they are from and why they are here. European Union (EU) nationals, for example, can work and study here and, with the exception of A8 nationals, generally have similar entitlements to UK nationals. People from outside the EU may be able to come to the UK on a student or au-pair visa, as a highly skilled worker or under special labour schemes. People may also be fleeing war or political oppression and come as asylum seekers. Once accepted as genuine refugees these people are given leave to remain. Within each of these categories there are a variety of statuses and entitlements that further complicate the picture.

'Once there were immigrants and refugees. Today there are unaccompanied minors, trafficked people, economic migrants, environmental refugees, asylum seekers, people with humanitarian protection, full refugee status and no doubt more' – Vaughan Jones, Praxis, *Connect*, Issue 22, p.12

Migrants have a wide range of support needs. Some speak good English and can readily adapt to life in the UK. Others are unfamiliar with the UK system and need support to integrate. It is often the more vulnerable groups that are likely to present to homelessness services while language and cultural barriers can make accessing services more difficult. Some may suffer from mental health problems, in the case of asylum seekers and refugees perhaps because of traumatic experiences in their home countries. A number of issues that make migrants, refugees and asylum seekers vulnerable to homelessness are discussed below.

Migrants have a wide range of support needs

Asylum seekers and refugees

The majority of asylum seekers are housed on a no-choice basis through the National Asylum Support Service (NASS) contracts. Accepted refugees on the other hand are generally eligible for social housing and benefits on the same basis as UK nationals.

Refugees leaving NASS accommodation

Many refugees paradoxically find themselves homeless at the stage when they are granted refugee status and become entitled to the same support as UK nationals. Once given 'leave to remain' individuals are generally required to leave NASS accommodation within 28 days. Sometimes if they have been housed in temporary accommodation this can be reduced to as little as 7 days. Finding accommodation within such a short period of time can be difficult for anyone. Without employment, family to fall back on, difficulties in being accepted as in priority need by HPUs and with delays in processing benefit claims many people end up homeless as a result.

Failed asylum seekers

People whose asylum claims are refused who are temporarily unable to return to their home countries should be supported under Section 4 of the Immigration and Asylum Act. They have to satisfy at least one of five criteria to qualify for support:

⇨ Taking steps to leave the UK but need time to complete arrangements.

⇨ Unable to leave because of a medical or physical impediment e.g. latter stages of a pregnancy.

⇨ No viable route to return is available

⇨ Have applied for judicial review and been granted permission to proceed.

⇨ To avoid a breach of the Human Rights Act 1998.

Economic migrants

A8 nationals

When the EU expanded in 2004, limitations were placed on the entitlement to state support of citizens from eight of the ten new countries, Poland, Lithuania, Estonia, Latvia, Slovenia, Slovakia, Hungary and the Czech Republic. Nationals from these so-called Accession 8 (A8) countries can come here to work but with limited entitlement to social provisions and benefits. Most workers are required to register on the Worker Registration Scheme. They can be entitled to certain benefits (e.g. child, housing and council tax benefit) and tax credits as soon as they are in work and registered but have to remain in continuous work for 12 months to get out-of-work benefits such as job seeker's allowance. While individuals are seeking work their right to reside in the UK is conditional on them being self-sufficient and not placing a burden on the social assistance system.

⇨ The above information is reprinted with kind permission from Homeless Link. For more information, please visit their website at www.homeless.org.uk

Homeless people's health

Information from St Mungo's

Homeless people are much more likely to be mentally and physically ill than the rest of the population. Many went on the street because they were mentally ill, or were heavy drinkers or drug addicts; others will have developed these problems while sleeping rough. This article looks at their problems, and St Mungo's response.

Physical health problems

⇨ People sleeping rough have a rate of physical health problems that is two or three times greater than in the general population.

⇨ These problems include: chronic chest and breathing problems, wounds and skin complaints, musculo-skeletal problems and digestive problems.

⇨ The rate of tuberculosis among rough sleepers and hostel residents is 200 times that of the known rate among the general population.

⇨ Rough sleepers aged between 45 and 64 have a death rate 25 times that of the general population.

(St Mungo's helps those with physical health problems by ensuring they see a GP, and by employing resident nurses and visiting doctors.)

Mental health problems

⇨ The Government's Social Exclusion Unit estimates that 30 to 50 per cent of people sleeping rough suffer from mental health problems, which, for about 88 per cent, existed before they went on the street.

(St Mungo's helps people with mental health disorders by ensuring they can see a GP and psychiatrist. We also employ a specialist mental health team which assesses residents and ensures appropriate treatment. We use the services of counsellors where appropriate.)

Drug and alcohol problems

⇨ About half of people sleeping rough are heavy drinkers and about one in seven are drug addicts.

(St Mungo's helps people with drink and drug problems by ensuring they can see a GP. We also employ a specialist alcohol and drug team which assesses residents and ensures appropriate treatment. We run a specialist detoxification unit and a special unit for drug users.)

⇨ The above information is reprinted with kind permission from St Mungo's. Visit www.mungos.org to view notes on this text or for more information.

© St Mungo's

Alcohol and drugs

Information from Resource Information Service

Many homeless people also have problems which are related to alcohol and drug misuse. In some cases, this actually contributes to their homelessness and difficulties with finding accommodation. Whilst there are community alcohol and drug services, not all are accessible to homeless people or geared to their needs. *Home and Dry? Homelessness and Substance Use* is a report examining the links between homelessness and substance use.

Homeless people with complex drug and/or alcohol problems face particular difficulties in finding accommodation or help and support to meet their needs. Many hostels are reluctant to accept homeless people with drug or alcohol problems. Those with Dual Diagnosis who also experience mental health problems have particularly severe difficulties in finding somewhere to stay or appropriate support services.

Historically, most services have been developed based on a therapeutic approach involving detox and abstinence. In recent years, some homelessness organisations have developed day and residential services (such as wet hostels), using a harm minimisation model that recognises that some individuals will continue to drink or take drugs.

The national drugs strategy Tackling Drugs Changing Lives, updated in 2002, aims to reduce the harm that drugs cause society. The government's drugs website contains a wealth of information on the strategy, including a section on homelessness. The harm caused by alcohol misuse is addressed in a separate strategy produced in March 2004. The Alcohol Harm Reduction Strategy for England is available from the Department of Health website, along with a range of other alcohol-related reports and statistics.

The National Treatment Agency for Substance Misuse (NTA) was set up in 2001 to increase the effectiveness of treatment for drug misuse in England. The NTA website includes an online directory of residential rehabilitation services in England and Wales for adult drug and alcohol misusers.

⇨ The above information is reprinted with kind permission from Resource Information Service. Visit www.homelesspages.org.uk for more information.

© Resource Information Service

The hidden homeless

A homeless person doesn't always fit into a category or match a stereotype. 'Hidden homelessness' describes people who move from place to place without having a fixed place to call home

A person trapped in hidden homelessness also covers people living in:

⇨ Friends' places;
⇨ Squats;
⇨ B&Bs;
⇨ Hostels;
⇨ Temporary accommodation;
⇨ Refuges;
⇨ Insecure accommodation – anyone who's being subjected to harassment within their household;
⇨ Inadequate accommodation – overcrowding, unsafe/run-down houses, people living without central heating, and people at risk of imminent eviction.

How common is hidden homelessness?

Hidden homelessness is said to affect around 4,000 people in Britain and is most common in people aged between 16 and 25. It's difficult to place an exact figure on the hidden homeless because many people who don't have a base of their own aren't necessarily sleeping on the streets. This means they won't be registered by their local authority as being homeless.

Nearly 7,000 young people are listed as high priority for housing within local councils. Shelter says that the problem is growing and over 15,000 young people a year are approaching its aid centres for housing help.

How do young people find themselves homeless?

Young people rarely choose to leave home without having a safe alternative. Still, many are forced out of their homes due to violent, sexual or racial abuse, poverty and family conflict.

By Julia Pearlman

There are a number of reasons why young people become homeless. Family and relationship breakdowns are the most common factor. Other issues that can create a barrier to someone not being in permanent accommodation include:

⇨ Unemployment;
⇨ Drug and alcohol problems;
⇨ Mental health problems;
⇨ Young offenders struggling to get work;
⇨ Young people leaving care;
⇨ Low self-esteem.

One in 12 young people are more likely to get sick because of bad housing and are more likely to be injured due to badly designed homes or dangerous fittings

The Big Issue's 2004 Audit revealed that 33% of its vendors were homeless before the age of 20.

'There are quite a lot of services available to the homeless but many people don't know how to access them and that's something we need to address,' says Keith Smith at *The Big Issue North*. 'Being homeless is much more complicated than not having a roof over your head. People who are homeless often have complex and varied needs.'

Living in inadequate housing can have a negative effect on health. One in 12 young people are more likely to get sick because of bad housing and are more likely to be injured due to badly designed homes or dangerous fittings. Young homeless people are also likely to miss up to a quarter of their schooling.

Help for the hidden homeless

There are a large number of charities based all over the UK that provide care, shelter and advice for homeless people. Centrepoint, Shelter and Banardo's specialise in youth homelessness. The YMCA also offers shelters or foyers for temporary accommodation.

'The first thing you should do is contact your local homelessness charity straight away. Even if they don't have bed spaces available,

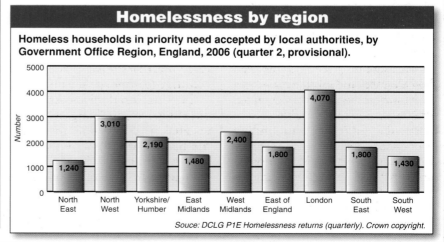

Homelessness by region

Homeless households in priority need accepted by local authorities, by Government Office Region, England, 2006 (quarter 2, provisional).

Region	Number
North East	1,240
North West	3,010
Yorkshire/Humber	2,190
East Midlands	1,480
West Midlands	2,400
East of England	1,800
London	4,070
South East	1,800
South West	1,430

Souce: DCLG P1E Homelessness returns (quarterly). Crown copyright.

they can point you in the right direction and give you other ideas for support,' says Amanda at Arch, a charity dedicated to preventing and resolving homelessness in North Staffordshire.

Charlette is 23 and has been living in temporary accommodation since the age of 15. 'Be strong because there's always a light at the end of the tunnel. There are other people out there to help you, so don't feel that you're alone. If I'd known about Crisis when I first became homeless I would have been a lot happier,' she says.

Hidden homelessness is said to affect around 4,000 people in Britain and is most common in people aged between 16 and 25

'I wish I'd put my head down and studied more, rather than wasting all that time. I was working from the age of 15 and making money instead of studying and working towards my goals. I didn't really know what I wanted to do when I was younger, but I'm getting there in the end!'

What's being done to help the hidden homeless?

Foyer
'There's a big lack of social housing and appropriate accommodation for people with complex needs. Young people often come to live in a foyer following a period of moving from one place to another or staying with friends, which is a classic example of hidden homelessness,' says Sophie Livingstone at Foyer.

'Many young people have said that if only they'd have known how hard it would be to live independently they would have thought twice about leaving home.'

Shelter
Shelter says that although the Government has done a lot to address street homelessness, there's actually been a steady increase in the number of families living in temporary accommodation, which continues to rise.

'People living in hostels can be moved on at any time and this means having to change schools, doctors, and getting used to new communities,' says Emma Guise at Shelter. 'We're calling on the government to take the problem seriously and commit to building more social housing because there just aren't enough social homes being built.'

Crisis
Crisis says that although there is a lot of positive work being done, it's not always easy for homeless people to reach out for help in order to get what they need.

'People living in hostels are often trapped there for years and years. They are unable to hold down a job, move into education and get their own home,' says Lucy Maggs at Crisis. 'At Crisis it's far more about finding a roof for someone. Homelessness is very isolating and demoralising. We provide activities and workshops to help people gain not only educational skills, but life skills to help them re-engage in society.'

⇨ The above information is reprinted with kind permission from TheSite.org. Visit www.thesite.org for more information.

© TheSite.org

Youth homelessness statistics

Every night Centrepoint provides a place to stay for over 500 homeless young people in its 16 London services, foyers and supported flats

Every young person who comes to Centrepoint provides us with information relating to their background and their reasons for becoming homeless. Here we outline some key statistics compiled from this information.

⇨ Each year, over 70% of the young people we see have slept rough.

⇨ Each year, over 40% of the young people we see have no qualifications at all.

⇨ 32% of the young people we see have run away from home aged 16 or 17.

⇨ Over 80% of the young people we see left home due to 'push factors' – conflicts, family breakdowns, evictions, abuse.

⇨ 21% of the young people we assist have been looked after by a local authority.

⇨ 57% of the young people we assist are black or of ethnic origin, however only 5% of the total UK population are black or of ethnic origin.

⇨ 24% of the young people we see have no source of income, and cannot support themselves when they first come to us.

⇨ The above information is reprinted with kind permission from Centrepoint. Visit www.centrepoint.org.uk for more information.

© Centrepoint

How does homelessness hurt?

Information from Housing Justice

Shelter estimates that over one million children in Britain are living in housing that damages their health, their education and their future. They live in damp, cold, infested housing; on estates ridden with fear and filth; at the whim of bad landlords; under the cloud of eviction and debt. At Housing Justice we agree that this is a national scandal. And the blame lies with a woefully inadequate housing system, incapable of providing the housing or the help that families need.

Homelessness hurts health

'Multiple housing deprivation appears to pose a health risk that is of the same magnitude as smoking and, on average, greater than that posed by excessive alcohol consumption.' BMA 2003.

Children living in cramped accommodation experience disturbed sleep, poor diet, hyperactivity, bedwetting and soiling, aggression and higher rates of accidents and infectious diseases. Homeless children are twice as likely to be admitted to hospital, with high admissions rates for accidents and infectious diseases. Adolescent girls in particular are very concerned about the lack of privacy in situations where they are often required to share a room with parents as well as older or younger siblings.

Homelessness hurts social inclusion

Poor housing in childhood is a major cause of adult poverty. The children spend the rest of their lives running to catch up. Children miss, on average, 55 school days (a quarter of a school year) due to the disruption of moves into and between temporary accommodation. This is on top of the difficulties of finding suitable places to do homework, and particularly

Christian vision in action **HOUSING JUSTICE**

the project and course work which is such a vital part of GCSEs. But exclusion includes exclusion from after-school activities and youth clubs, as well as from school itself. Children are further restricted by the lack of outside play areas. The problem with outdoor spaces includes fear of violence as well as lack of suitable space.

Today there are over 1.5million fewer social housing (council/ housing association) homes than 25 years ago

---

Homelessness hurts friendships

It is very difficult to leave friends behind – and to make new ones – especially if you don't know how long you will be staying in a place. Children are aware of the lack or poor quality of 'amenities' in their temporary accommodation – especially the toilets. This makes it very difficult for them to build up friendships by inviting people back to their home. To make it worse, they are often bullied at school.

Another difficult loss is pets. Families usually have to get rid of your pets when they lose their home… 'My cat's gone to Battersea …when we get a new house we'll get her back.' (Girl, 4)

The case for more (affordable) homes for families

Today there are over 1.5million fewer social housing (council/ housing association) homes than 25 years ago. Meanwhile, housing costs are a significant poverty trap. High-cost housing leads to high levels of overcrowding, homelessness and rising numbers of people in temporary accommodation. Nationally only 50% of working households can afford to buy even the lowest-price accommodation (in London this falls to 24%). The solution lies in greater investment in social housing.

Two changes that would help homeless young people…

⇨ Reform of the rule that means young people living on benefit and in education lose entitlement to income support on their 19th birthday. This would ensure young people were able to complete their studies rather than drop out in order to seek work immediately.

⇨ Extend the prohibition on the long-term use of B&B accommodation to 16- and 17-year olds.

⇨ The above information is reprinted with kind permission from Housing Justice. Visit www.justhousing.org.uk for more information.

© Housing Justice

Too much, too young

Problem debt amongst homeless young people

Introduction

At a time when rising debt levels are causing concern for society, government and individuals this article examines the scale and extent of debt amongst homeless young people, one of the most vulnerable groups in society. It is underpinned by a more detailed report available at www.centrepoint.org. Over 100 young people were consulted for this research. This report reflects their views and experiences, and those of the staff who work closely with them.

For some young people, debt is a considerable individual burden and the large-scale impact of this can have much wider social consequences working against efforts of government and other agencies to prevent and tackle social exclusion. Eighty-two per cent of the homeless young people surveyed are in debt, owing £1,000 on average, but as much as £15,000 in one case. The Government is currently considering measures to tackle the problem of debt amongst groups such as these. Its success or failure will depend on whether or not it can reach those most susceptible to debt, preventing unmanageable debt and giving people the tools to manage their finances.

Consequences

The most common consequence of being over-indebted is stress and illness. Some of the young people interviewed are being treated for depression as a result of their debt. A third say they are not coping with the level of debt they have.

A common theme amongst homeless young people is the importance of having hope that life will be more stable in the future. Some young people believe they are prevented from a better future because they owe money they cannot repay.

Confidence and resilience are key factors in learning to live independently. Some young people

see their debt as evidence that they are a failure, and this can prevent them from gaining confidence, building up resilience and moving out of homelessness.

Causes

There is a distinction between people who will not pay back their debts, those who genuinely cannot pay and those who could pay given the right help and support. The research found that homeless young people overwhelmingly fall into the latter two categories, with the majority able to repay debts but only at an appropriate level and with the right support.

Credit is important to homeless young people because they often live on low incomes and incur more expenses than young people living with their parents, but because of a lack of assets and a sporadic income many homeless young people are caught up in a spiral of debt repayments and borrowing.

There are five key reasons why young people who are homeless or at risk of homelessness fall into this trap.

Making ends meet

Seventeen per cent of the young people questioned for Centrepoint's research said a low income was the main reason they had got into debt.

'I never used the overdraft until I lost my job and I was a little bit hard up. You get your benefits which are enough mostly, but things wear out. It's not so much being irresponsible, but if you're not working you don't have anything else.'

Managing on a low income is exacerbated for those who are also repaying high levels of debt. This is causing extreme hardship for some young people. Eighteen per cent of young people in the survey have less than £30 a week to live on after meeting debt repayments.

High levels of debt repayment force some young people to borrow more, causing further hardship. Four per cent of young people in the survey repay more each week than their weekly income, so have to borrow more to do so. A third of respondents say they have tried to pay off existing debts by borrowing more. This may reflect a lack of access to affordable credit and the difficulties young

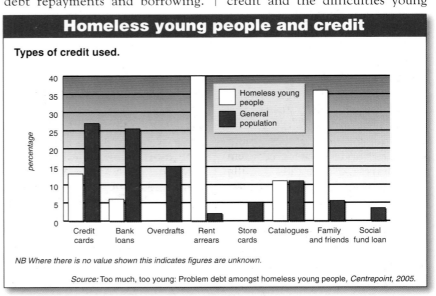

Homeless young people and credit

Types of credit used.

NB Where there is no value shown this indicates figures are unknown.

Source: Too much, too young: Problem debt amongst homeless young people, Centrepoint, 2005.

people have negotiating affordable repayment rates with lenders.

Twenty-seven per cent of the young people surveyed are over-indebted compared to 7% of the total population. While it is unsurprising that socially excluded young people are more likely to be over-indebted, the results are quite striking: 23% are repaying more than a quarter of their weekly income in debt repayments, compared to 5% of the total population.

Benefits

Young people with a low or no income can be pushed into debt by poor benefit administration. This is cited as the main cause of debt by 5% of homeless young people, but mentioned as a factor by many more. A fast and accurate benefits system is an essential precondition for reducing overindebtedness.

'It was too many things at once which left me with no safety net.'

Jamilla has been homeless since her relationship with her boyfriend broke down and she lost her job. She is 23. She first got into debt because of incorrect benefits advice which delayed her JSA and housing benefit for several months. She lived on her overdraft and used her store card to withdraw cash for several months because she couldn't get any other credit. The company put her limit up without telling her, and she now owes them several thousand pounds. Jamilla is negotiating with debt collection agencies, and paying back a little every week. The experience has badly knocked her confidence. She wants to work but is finding it daunting: 'in the past I had the confidence to go out and get a new job, but as hard

as you try they can see you're not completely together'.

Young people who are homeless or at risk of homelessness need a housing benefit system that is fast and accurate to prevent the overpayments which cause debt, or being forced to borrow from elsewhere to cover their rent.

A third of the young people surveyed have wanted to get money advice but two-fifths of these have not managed to access any

---

The majority of young people surveyed think it is difficult to claim benefits. The benefits system can be very complex for young people because many benefits are subject to age restrictions. This complexity can cause delays in payment and mean that some young people are given incorrect advice. For example one young person was told to apply for the Working Tax Credit, but is ineligible because she is under 25.

'It was getting bad advice initially that did it for me.'

The DWP should provide more support, training and guidance amongst Jobcentre Plus staff regarding benefit entitlements for young people.

Information, education and advice

Centrepoint works with many young people who have poor competence in literacy, numeracy and financial literacy. Lack of any of these skills can be a major factor in whether young people get into debt, and whether they are able to prevent debts from escalating. For most young people borrowing is a way to achieve their goals, but unless they are able to manage their debt, it can become a factor which prevents them from building a better future.

Thirteen per cent of the young people Centrepoint works with have numeracy problems. Financial literacy is also poor amongst the

people surveyed; one-third do not know how to budget.

With increasing numbers of credit options on offer, financial literacy is becoming more important.

'They send you information about interest rates, but 1.6% doesn't mean anything to me. I need more information than that.'

Many young people consulted think financial education would be helpful. The Government's strategy to improve financial literacy will only work if it reaches disadvantaged groups and tackles the linked problems of poor numeracy and literacy. Homeless young people may have had interrupted or poor attendance at school, and could be better reached through youth groups or sixth form colleges.

A third of the young people surveyed have wanted to get money advice but two-fifths of these have not managed to access any. The Government and Financial Services Authority (FSA) are drawing up a strategy to improve financial capability which considers young people as a distinct group. This is appropriate because some young people have particular concerns and fears about accessing advice.

Young people need easy access to good, personalised money services. Specialist money advice for all ages, including the national debtline, must ensure they can respond to the needs of young people. Local advice services are important to homeless young people because they find it very hard to find money for travel.

Affordable credit

The types of debt amongst homeless young people tend to reflect the type of credit they can access. Only 13% have credit card debts and 7% have bank loans. A third of the homeless young people questioned had difficulties in accessing credit of any kind.

Mail order catalogues (12%) are an attractive form of borrowing for many homeless young people because they provide goods immediately but have typically higher prices than on the high street. This appears to be the case for young parents in particular, who cannot always wait to buy things their children need.

Others seek out more informal sources of borrowing. A number of young people in the survey owe money to friends or relatives – 37%, compared to 6% of the total population. Many homeless young people spend long periods of time sleeping on friends' floors because they have nowhere else to go. Support networks can also be the critical factor in whether people are able to escape homelessness. Borrowing can place strain on relationships, or at the most extreme it can destroy them.

The Government has recognised that credit is integral to modern living, but it can be even more important for homeless young people who have to afford rent deposits, and buy essentials, like an oven or fridge, to set up home, but do not have families to help them. Some young people have taken out expensive loans or are using store cards, with a typical APR of 29% to access cash because they have been turned down for overdrafts or credit cards.

Current affordable credit options like credit unions are not widely understood by the young people consulted and are difficult for them to access because they often operate on the principle that you have to pay in before you can borrow. In addition homeless young people may be barred from accessing them because they do not belong to a workplace or local community; common criteria for entry. It may be appropriate for organisations working with homeless people to explore the feasibility of setting up a credit union to overcome these problems of access.

Being young

Young people are very susceptible to promotional literature advertising financial products. Student discounts, glossy brochures and offers of clothes, shoes and music which are buy-now, pay-later are very tempting. Homeless young people may be more susceptible to these things because many cannot afford these products, even occasionally. Many young people regret having taken up these offers at a younger age when they did not fully understand the

consequences or have the maturity to assess the risks. Staff echo this concern.

'Is it right to give young people at that age so much power? They [lenders] are making an assumption that they can manage. It's clear that some of them can't' – Centrepoint support and development worker.

Two-thirds of the young people consulted for this research have been sent promotional literature encouraging them to take out credit

---

In light of this, it is of concern that young people are sent so much promotional literature offering them incentives to take out credit. Two-thirds of the young people consulted for this research have been sent promotional literature encouraging them to take out credit. Of greater concern is the significant minority of young people who have been sent promotional literature after becoming homeless. A fifth of the young people in the survey say they have received letters inviting them to apply for credit since they became homeless and moved into a hostel.

The Financial Services Authority (FSA) code states that care should be taken with young people. However, there is at present no code to cover the marketing of products. It would be beneficial if the DTI were to draw up specific guidelines for lending to young people, which would cover

the way these products should be marketed to them. Given the FSA's expertise in this area, they may be the most appropriate body to do this.

'Some young people don't know how to research it at all. Why would they? They've never had credit cards before. They don't know to look at the APR' – Centrepoint support and development worker.

In addition, some lenders put up credit limits without the young person requesting it. Homeless young people may have moved several times and do not always receive letters informing them, calling into question the transparency of the process. Several young people interviewed had got into a spiral of high interest repayments by using store cards or overdrafts without realising their limit had gone up.

'Why do they let you go over your overdraft? I didn't ask them for the money. They shouldn't give it to you. The more you spend the more they put your credit up. If they can see you're not managing they should stop.'

In reality the benefits for young people and lenders are illusory, creating debt that is unmanageable for the former and unrecoverable for the latter. Giving young people higher credit limits they have not asked for loosens their control over their finances with serious consequences.

⇨ The above information is an extract from the Centrepoint briefing paper *Too much, too young – Problem debt amongst homeless young people* and is reprinted with permission. Visit www.centrepoint.org.uk to view the entire text and footnotes, or for more information.

© Centrepoint

Mental health and youth homelessness

Mental health problems prevalent among young homeless people in London, yet services are inadequate, says new report

According to a new report released today by the Mental Health Foundation and Centrepoint, the increasing numbers of young homeless people with mental health problems are not getting adequate support because services rarely work together to provide the necessary help.

Over two-thirds (69%) of the young homeless people aged 16-25 surveyed for the report have mental health problems. Half (50%) experience regular feelings of anxiety and depression as a result of being homeless, and a fifth (19%) had received a psychiatric diagnosis for schizophrenia, bi-polar disorder or clinical depression prior to becoming homeless. Of those, half (10%) were forced to leave the family home because of their mental health problem.

The report, *Making the Link between Mental Health and Youth Homelessness*, claims that despite these figures staff working within housing and youth homelessness services lack the necessary skills to deal with mental health issues and need specialist training. They also struggle to access appropriate support for young people experiencing mental distress. Mental health assessment waiting times are long and this lack of early intervention leaves young people vulnerable to developing more entrenched mental health problems. As a result young people often reach crisis point before being seen by a mental health team.

> ## Over two-thirds (69%) of the young homeless people aged 16-25 surveyed for the report have mental health problems

The report highlights that some voluntary sector housing and homelessness support services encounter barriers when trying to refer young people to the statutory sector. This is because mental health services are underresourced and some statutory services are reluctant to accept referrals from the voluntary sector. The research also found that young people with both mental health and drug and alcohol problems often do not get the help they need because services rarely work together making it difficult to provide complete care packages.

Moira Fraser, Head of Policy at the Mental Health Foundation, said:

'There are a few services in London who do deliver integrated mental health and homelessness care but it is rare. We need to see more services working in unison and better pathways to specialist mental health and drug and alcohol services for young homeless people. Vulnerable young people asking for help should not have to face long waiting lists or have to cope with services that aren't able to deliver.'

Balbir Chatrik, Director of Policy at Centrepoint, said:

'The last few years have seen the growing complexity of mental health issues affecting homeless young people including self-harm and addiction, yet access to mental health services remains limited. In 2002 Centrepoint established its own Health Team to provide dedicated and integrated support to young people in Centrepoint services. Our experience shows that it is vital to get services working together in order to provide help before crisis point is reached.'

Almost half of the young people surveyed (45%) became homeless because they were forced to leave their family home due to a breakdown in family relations most often because of the young person's behaviour connected to their experience of drug use, criminal activity or mental ill health. A fifth (20%) chose to leave their family home, others found themselves homeless as refugees seeking asylum in the UK (14%).

The charities make a number of recommendations in the report. First among these is a call for joined-up commissioning of integrated services across sectors, and for mechanisms to enable rapid access to specialist mental health and drug and alcohol services when needed by young people.

25 July 2006

⇨ Reproduced from the Mental Health Foundation website with their permission. For the most up-to-date information, please visit www.mentalhealth.org.uk

Preventing homelessness

This article looks at different ways in which the problem of homelessness can be prevented. We are all familiar with the saying prevention is better than cure

The 2002 Homelessness Act

A major step towards preventing homelessness was taken with the introduction in England and Wales of the 2002 Homelessness Act. This put new duties on local authorities to tackle homelessness at the strategic level and work as much as possible to prevent people becoming homeless, rather than managing the emergency situation once people have lost their homes.

The first step taken by councils under the Act was to review the level of homelessness in the area so that they had an understanding of the causes and extent of the existing problem. Other organisations, such as local homelessness charities, housing advice centres and other relevant council departments, also had an input into the review. The councils used the information on the problem to compile a homelessness strategy to tackle the existing and future problem for the area. The homelessness strategy provides a framework for policy dealing with the homelessness problem and for preventing future homelessness.

Government analysis of the homelessness strategies produced by the 354 local authorities in England and 22 local authorities in Wales shows that all strategies stressed the benefits of preventing homelessness – councils acknowledge that it is far better to invest in preventative work than to have to provide emergency housing at short notice when people are literally roofless. They can also see that prevention saves money – it is far more cost effective to pay a small amount to keep someone in their home than to pay out for temporary accommodation costs.

In the best councils, adoption of the homelessness strategies has led to a culture change in the organisation and a shifting of resources from responding to preventing the problem of homelessness. In all councils the process of compiling the strategy meant that for the first time homelessness and homelessness prevention have been dealt with at the strategic level.

Sustainable communities: settled homes, changing lives

The importance of prevention was emphasised by the government in its five-year housing strategy *Sustainable communities: settled homes, changing lives* released in March 2005. This sets out the government's priorities in tackling homelessness in England for the period to 2010.

National homelessness strategy for Wales

The Welsh national homelessness strategy published in December 2005 stresses the importance of preventing homelessness. It directs local authorities and homelessness services to direct their attention to preventing homelessness first and only to follow the procedure for re-housing homeless people the preventative efforts have failed.

What do we mean by preventing homelessness?

'Preventing homelessness means providing people with the ways and means to address their housing and other needs in order to avoid homelessness. Prevention activities include those which enable a household to remain in their current home, where appropriate, or to enable a planned and timely move and help sustain independent living.' Office of the Deputy Prime Minister – *Sustainable Communities: settled homes; changing lives.*

What's the best way to prevent homelessness?

Homelessness can be prevented by a variety of different interventions to tackle the problem before it reaches crisis point. For homelessness prevention to work, early intervention is vital. Research into homelessness shows that housing problems do not suddenly appear but develop over time.

There is often a period of up to four or five months between the first indication of a housing problem and the eviction notice being served. Traditionally a council housing department would only intervene in a situation when it was reaching crisis point – i.e. when the family had received an eviction notice and were given 28 days' notice to vacate the property. As a result of the focus on prevention, councils should be geared up to intervene in a housing problem soon after it develops. Often councils will develop links with landlords and other bodies and work with them to identify problems as they develop and so prevent the problem spiralling out of control. Understanding the landlords, and the tenants' circumstances, needs and desires can go a long way towards preventing homelessness.

Housing advice and information

Housing advice, as provided by the Housing Justice Alliance of Housing Advice Centres, empowers people by providing them with objective information and advice on their housing options and services available to them. In addition, centres can give advice on other problems, such as debt and benefit issues which often are the cause of housing problems. Housing advice centres can also contact landlords and other organisations on the tenant's behalf and try to resolve the problem. Housing advice centres break down the (often arbitrary) distinctions that are made between statutory, non-statutory, intentional and unintentional homelessness.

For homelessness prevention to work, early intervention is vital. Research into homelessness shows that housing problems do not suddenly appear but develop over time

---

Rent deposit schemes

To move in to housing in the private rented sector an individual usually requires a deposit of a least one month's rent as well as a month's rent in advance. This is unaffordable to most people without large savings – more than £1,000 might be required depending on the area. Those who are homeless or are threatened with homelessness are unlikely to have savings to fall back upon to pay for this which means they are unable to move into private rented accommodation. Rent deposit schemes pay the deposit to the landlord enabling homeless people or those threatened with homelessness to take out a private sector tenancy.

Often rent deposit schemes will be available to everyone – including people who do not fall into one of the priority need categories. The involvement of an external body should also help to overcome any fears the landlord might have in letting their property to a homeless person. Many of the members of the Housing Justice Alliance of Housing Advice Centres pioneered the use of rent deposit schemes – housing advice centres such as Kingston, Kirklees and Oswestry have for a number of years helped people move into long-term private sector property.

Tenancy support

Tenancy support is a broad term used to describe services that exist to help people into housing and once in ensure that they do not lose it. These services range from providing furniture and other household essentials when someone moves into a new house, advice on utilities, budgeting and navigating local services, to help with finding treatment for drug or alcohol problems. Specialist tenancy support services are available for people with mental health problems, ex-offenders and long-term homeless people. Anti-social behaviour by tenants can be tackled in this way too – with the aim of stopping it or moving tenants before the landlord starts court proceedings. If tenants find they get into difficulties, tenancy support services can intervene with the landlord or other organisation to work out a way to resolve the problem before it gets to the desperate stage when eviction is threatened.

Landlords' services

As well as looking after tenants local authority housing departments can also run landlord support services to provide information for existing and prospective private landlords on what they should expect from tenants and what they are required to do to comply with landlord and tenant law. These aim to prevent unnecessary court proceedings on both sides and ensure that landlords and tenants are able to have a business-like relationship.

One council in the South of England with a large private rented sector has a team of housing department staff whose sole duty is ensuring that landlords are happy with arrangements – recently, tenants came to the Council with

an eviction notice after the landlord told them he was selling the house. On investigation by the landlords' team the true story emerged – the landlord actually wanted to increase his rents and thought that the only way he could do it was by evicting the tenants and taking on new ones paying higher rents. The landlords' team was able to give him details of the procedure to increase rents in compliance with the law, and so the tenants agreed to pay a higher rent enabling them to remain in their family home.

Prevention funds

Often linked to tenancy support services, some local authorities have set aside small homelessness prevention funds which are available to housing officers to help families who are facing homelessness as a result of a (relatively) small financial problem such as rental arrears. These funds allow local authority Housing

Officers to think creatively around a problem and apply unconventional solutions to prevent homelessness.

To prevent homelessness we need to be building more homes

One London borough allocates a notional £200 from its prevention fund to Housing Officers for every family they are helping. This money can be freely spent by the Housing Officer; for example, in one case it was used to clear a small rent arrear that had built up and which was preventing a family accessing a private or council tenancy. In another case the money was used to arrange for gardening work to be done for an older person who was threatened with eviction because he was unable to maintain the garden. In another case the money was used to pay for travel tickets so that a family could move to a new area where they had relatives and where there was suitable private sector accommodation. The thinking behind the funding is that spending a few hundred pounds now to prevent a problem or provide a solution is better than spending £400+ a week for the family in temporary accommodation.

Mediation
Mediation services attempt to resolve problems resulting from relationship breakdowns either between parents and young people or between adults sharing housing. Usually mediators are called in when the relationship has broken down and one of the people has been made homeless – often, young people might be thrown out of their parents' home following an argument – or they are threatened with homelessness.

Mediators act as impartial facilitators for meetings between the affected parties so that differences can be discussed and hopefully resolved, and the affected people either resume living together harmoniously or, if they decide that the relationship has broken down irretrievably, they can seek alternative accommodation. If

this occurs, hopefully the mediation service will have enabled them to consider their options and attempted to resolve some of the issues in the breakup of the relationship. Mediation services are usually provided by independent charities with funding from local authority housing departments.

Domestic violence/abuse
One situation where mediation is not appropriate is domestic violence or an abusive situation. Usually in these circumstances the relationship has broken down to such an extent that mediation is not possible or desirable.

Traditionally council housing departments would, as a matter of priority, re-house victims of domestic violence outside the area. This has an impact on the whole family, as children will be forced to change schools and face other disruption which impacts on their whole lives. When questioned, researchers found that 60% of women re-housed as a result of domestic violence stated that they would prefer to remain in their own homes. As a result, 'sanctuary' schemes have been developed across the country which bring together the police, the housing department and other relevant authorities to develop solutions which will allow the family to continue living in their home. The council can arrange to provide increased security measures on the home such as strengthening doors and locks, installing alarms and a secure means of contacting the police. In addition, the police can start legal proceedings against the violent partner to prevent them coming near the house. The family is therefore able to stay in the home and not have their lives disrupted by the violent partner.

Longer-term solutions to prevent homelessness – build more homes
In the long term to prevent homelessness we need to be building more homes for sale and for rent so that people are able to choose decent housing of an appropriate size for themselves and their families. This will avoid many of the issues that give rise to stress that can lead to relationship breakdown and homelessness.

In 2006 house building is at an historic low. In order to begin to address the mismatch between housing demand and supply a government economist, Kate Barker, in 2004 estimated that we need to build an extra 140,000 new homes a year for the next 20 years. Of these 140,000 it was recommended that at least 23,000 should be affordable social housing to begin to replace the 1.5 million homes sold to tenants under the right-to-buy policy since 1979. Once sold, these homes were not replaced.

Plans are currently under way to build more housing each year, including 30,000 extra homes in the South East. This is a welcome attempt to begin to address the severe shortage of housing in South East England. Inevitably, some housing will have to be built on greenfield sites, but most people would agree that the trade-off between the loss of a small amount of countryside and ensuring that people are adequately housed is worth it.

In December 2005 the government announced its response to the conclusions of Kate Barker's review of housing supply. It took on board many of her arguments and pledged to increase housing supply by 50,000 new homes year. It also pledged to increase the number of new social housing homes making it a priority for the 2007 spending review.

We need to ensure that the new housing developments are appropriate for the local need. So, for example, in areas with lots of families in housing need, we should ensure that new developments are of homes suitable for families of varying sizes rather than simply one- and two-bedroom flats. In an area with older people in housing need the reverse is true as they will probably prefer smaller homes. In addition we need to ensure that the infrastructure such as transport, community facilities, schools is in place and suitable for the area. Only when we have all this in place will we be able to build truly sustainable communities.

⇨ Information from Housing Justice. Visit www.justhousing.org.uk for more information.

© Housing Justice

Where to get help

There are a number of organisations that help people sleeping on the streets. They have specialist knowledge of the problems you may have and the services available. Some organisations have staff to help people with drug, alcohol or mental health problems

The services for people sleeping on the streets are based mainly in cities and large towns. Rural areas also have services, but they may be more limited. Use the Advice Services Directory to find an agency that can tell you what is available in your area, which might include:

⇨ Day centres
⇨ Soup runs
⇨ Outreach teams
⇨ Hostels and nightshelters
⇨ Resettlement teams.

Day centres

Day centres are places that people sleeping on the streets can go to during the day. People who have left the streets can also use them for activities and companionship even if they are living in their own homes.

The services provided by each day centre vary, as do their opening times. Most do not open at weekends or in the evening. Generally, day centres provide:

⇨ cheap or free food
⇨ laundry room
⇨ washing facilities
⇨ activities
⇨ advice on finding accommodation and benefits
⇨ access to medical treatment.

Shelter

Soup runs

In some areas, agencies distribute free food and drinks to people sleeping on the streets. They usually visit certain areas at specific times of the evening and/or early morning.

Outreach teams

Not all areas have outreach teams. In some areas, they are known as Contact and Assessment Teams (CATs). Some areas have outreach teams attached to day centres. They work on the street. They advise people how to find accommodation and may help them to get it. They can also help with claiming benefits.

Hostels and nightshelters

Hostels and nightshelters provide housing for people sleeping on the streets.

Hostel accommodation can be:
⇨ temporary (on a daily basis or for one to six months)

⇨ permanent
⇨ supported (for people who are ready to move on to their own home)
⇨ high care (for people with medical needs).

Some hostels will accept people who turn up at the door. Other hostels need a referral from an agency. This could be a day centre or an outreach team. Vacancies fill quickly and once the hostel is full, people are turned away.

Accommodation varies from hostel to hostel. Residents might have their own room, they might share a room or they may sleep in dormitories. Some hostels are for certain groups of people, for example, young people, older people and people with mental health problems.

Generally, hostels provide:
⇨ meals or cooking facilities
⇨ laundry room
⇨ washing facilities
⇨ games/TV room.

You have to pay to stay, but the staff will help you apply for benefits.

Nightshelters are usually free. They are generally for short stays, usually a few days. People normally have to leave in the morning and can't return until the evening. If you want information about hostels and shelters that might be available in your area, use the accommodation search on Homeless UK's website.

Resettlement teams

Some hostels may have a resettlement worker or team. They can help to find longer-term housing. They may also help people to find work or a training scheme.

⇨ The above information is reprinted with kind permission from Shelter. Visit www.shelter.org.uk for more information.

© Shelter 2006

Helping the homeless

Is it right to give money to the homeless, or can it make the situation worse in the long run? Are you someone who delves into your pockets for your last bit of change without any hesitation, or do you refuse because you're worried it will be spent on alcohol or drugs?

How many times have you walked past someone shivering in a doorway begging for spare change or sat next to a cash point as you self-consciously draw out wads of cash for your big night out?

It's natural to feel guilty and want to help, but for many of us there's also the worry about whether they're legitimate. Is it kinder to offer money to people less fortunate than ourselves, or will we be doing more harm than good?

The many faces of homelessness

'Many people think that homeless people are lazy and should just go out and get a job,' says Amanda, at Arch, a charity dedicated to preventing and resolving homelessness in North Staffordshire. 'Nevertheless, people become homeless for a number of reasons – many of which aren't their own fault. They require long-term support, rather than condemnations.'

'They often have significant problems to deal with,' says Sophie Livingstone at Foyer. 'A common misconception is that it's your own fault if you've become homeless; that homeless people are alcoholics or drug users; and they are going to cause anti-social behaviour. I don't think people realise that it could happen to any of us and it's a much more common situation to find yourself in than you may realise.'

Still, in some cases, it seems we may be right to be suspicious. In April 2006 a team of professional beggars in Croydon were found to be travelling from one place to another earning £80 a day tax free simply by begging.

The police identified about 20 people, sometimes working in shifts, who were regularly working in the town centre, largely to fuel their

By Julia Pearlman

drug habits. Last year, Westminster Council revealed that more than £300,000 given to beggars over a period of two months in London was spent on drugs.

Possible solutions to the problem

1. Don't give money to beggars

Cities such as Aberdeen and Nottingham have been urging locals to use collection boxes rather than giving money directly to street beggars. The aim of the scheme is to put off aggressive beggars by encouraging people to use the boxes, which will then be distributed to homeless charities.

> **'Many people think that homeless people are lazy and should just go out and get a job'**

Councils involved in the project believe that if you cut off the source of the income, people will stop begging, but charities such as Shelter and Crisis argue that people shouldn't be told whether they can or can't give money to beggars.

'Obviously there may be issues about where the money may end up, but every person is different and it may be the case that these people need help to get food,' says Emma Guise at Shelter.

Keith Smith at *The Big Issue* agrees that it's not fair to tell people that they mus-tn't give money to beggars and encourages us to buy the magazine instead. 'We see buying *The Big Issue* as a positive alternative. All vendors are earning a legitimate

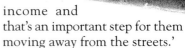

income and that's an important step for them moving away from the streets.'

The Killing with Kindness campaign has been launched to reduce the number of beggars and make life easier for local residents. 'We want to change people's behaviour, but not by attempting to punish beggars because they do deserve access to treatment and help. It's not easy because often these people are some of the most troubled and difficult people to assist, but everyone has different needs. New arrivals on the streets don't often know what's out there to help them,' says Natasha Bishopp, assistant director of Community Protection.

2. Treatment, housing programmes and support

The Reading Single Homeless Project, which launched at the end of 2005, targeted beggars by diverting homeless people into treatment and housing programmes. The scheme resulted in a 52% drop in the number of rough sleepers in Reading town centre. Nine of the 20 people sleeping rough in the area were housed, nine underwent drug treatment and five no longer need treatment.

Crisis has come up with the idea of 'Service Navigators'. These are individuals who are allocated to a homeless person so that they have an individual port of call though which

they can contact all the help, support and services they need.

3. *Getting tough*

Police around the country are tackling begging by handing out injunctions and anti-social behaviour orders. They hope it will prevent people sleeping rough, taking illegal drugs, and persistently begging within a certain distance of any cash-point or bank, or the town centre itself. Many beggars have been arrested and fined and offenders are warned that they'll face jail if they break the orders.

It's natural to feel guilty and want to help

How can you help?

The majority of organisations agree that even if you don't have much empathy with homeless people, by supporting agencies that are working to find long-term solutions to homelessness, you'll actually be helping to reduce the problems in your area.

The Big Issue is an example of how the public can help people make their own way. Its message, 'Working, not begging', epitomises the approach that the charity is trying to make and the way it's getting people into work.

The main message to us all is that ultimately it's up to you what you do with your cash. Often we want to see our money go directly to someone – it's a little bit like when you are at a restaurant and you put the tip in the waitress's hand rather than on the table, so as to avoid it being shared out, or worse, stolen.

Perhaps the next time you walk past a collection box you might want to donate your money directly to a homeless organisation or campaign. By doing this you could be helping agencies continue to support, train and house a large number of vulnerable people. Even if you can't afford to part with any money, simply by sparing some of your time volunteering through charities and local schemes, you could be an essential lifeline to those in desperate need of help.

If you're unsure about giving money directly to a homeless person, a welcome act of kindness could be to order an extra cup of tea when making your regular morning breakfast run before work. Although it's only short-term relief, a gesture such as this could make someone's day.

⇨ The above information is reprinted with kind permission from TheSite.org. For information on this and other issues, please visit www. thesite.org

© TheSite.org

Homelessness: key facts

Information from the Department for Communities and Local Government

The Government has made major progress in tackling the worst forms of homelessness. Rough sleeping is at a record low and we have ended the scandal of families living in bed and breakfast hotels for long periods. The next steps are to get more people into settled homes and out of temporary accommodation. 92 per cent of families with children living in temporary accommodation are in good quality self-contained homes, with their own kitchen, bathroom, and living space, but they do not have the security and opportunities a settled home brings.

The Government's homelessness strategy *Sustainable Communities: settled homes; changing lives* aims to halve the number of households living in temporary accommodation by 2010. We will achieve this by investing in more social housing, as well as increasing funding to prevent homelessness and building more homes across the board.

The Government is increasing the supply of new social homes by 50 per cent by 2008, providing 75,000 new social homes over the next three years. In addition, as part of the response to the Barker Review, the Government announced it would go further and make social housing a priority in the next spending review as well.

We are allocating more than £80 million to local authorities over the next two years to invest in further prevention schemes which have demonstrated considerable success. The latest National Statistics show a 27 per cent reduction in the number of households becoming homeless compared with the same period last year. This is the lowest number of new cases of homelessness at this time of year since 1985, and the latest in an overall downward trend in acceptances since the beginning of 2004. In additon, the number of households in temporary accommodation has also fallen below 100,000 for the first time since 2004.

⇨ The above information is reprinted with kind permission from the Department for Communities and Local Government. Visit www. communities.gov.uk for more information.

© Crown copyright

Missed opportunities

The case for investment in learning and skills for homeless people

The impact of learning and skills on homelessness

Homeless people often have a range of needs in addition to their need for a home. These needs both contribute to and are exacerbated by homelessness. This research found evidence that learning and skills make a positive contribution to all of these aspects of homeless people's needs. As well as increasing the skills of homeless people and improving their employability, engagement in learning and skills activities can also improve mental health and reduce problematic substance misuse or offending. These benefits were supported by wider research, and powerfully illustrated during the interviews with homeless people carried out during this study.

Needs of homeless people

⇨ 2% are in full-time work
⇨ 70% have mental health needs
⇨ 50-75% have a history of problematic substance misuse
⇨ 40% have a history of offending
⇨ 37% have no qualifications (compared to 10% of general population)

The Government has accepted that tackling the multiple needs of homeless people is essential if sustainable solutions to homelessness are to be found. Despite this, levels of repeat homelessness remain unacceptably high, as shown by the next statistics.

Experiences of homeless people

⇨ Two out of every three homeless people have been homeless more than once
⇨ One in ten have been homeless more than 10 times
⇨ A quarter have been homeless for more than five years
⇨ Two-thirds of rough sleepers have had tenancies in the past but lost them
⇨ Each tenancy breakdown costs housing authorities more than £2,000

Two out of every three homeless people have been homeless more than once

---

Through its Supporting People and Homelessness Prevention grant funding programmes the Government is encouraging housing authorities and homelessness agencies to develop and implement strategies for preventing homelessness. It has recently invested significant capital funding to upgrade and modernise hostels into places of change for homeless people, with the intention that 'meaningful activity' will be a key part of the services offered. Despite this, however, dedicated revenue funding has not been identified to enable hostel and day centre providers to provide these services. Although Supporting People funding can pay for the development of life skills, providers reported that in practice Supporting People administering authorities are cutting funding for this aspect of their work. In one case a provider has lost two-thirds of its Supporting People for life skills training, with no obvious alternative source available.

Engagement in learning and skills development helps to bring an end to homelessness in a number of ways.

⇨ It builds confidence and self-esteem – and through these the belief that positive change is possible.
⇨ It gives people structure, purpose and meaning in their lives – all of which are essential first steps to goal-setting and achievement.
⇨ It equips people with the skills necessary to interact successfully both in work and non-work settings – and thereby their chances of ending their social exclusion.
⇨ It tackles boredom and widens social networks – thereby helping individuals to leave behind negative past behaviours and peer influences.
⇨ It improves the ability to access and make use of services – thereby increasing independence and ensuring that wider needs are more likely to be met.
⇨ It improves employability – and thereby the chance of ending financial exclusion.

Many homeless people fear that they have neither the life skills (for instance money management, ability to deal with agencies, communication

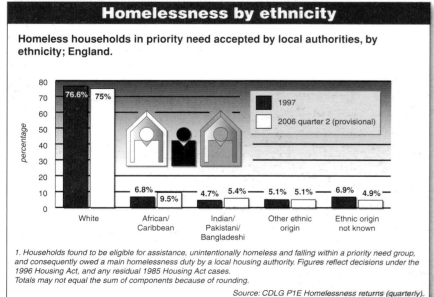

Homelessness by ethnicity

Homeless households in priority need accepted by local authorities, by ethnicity; England.

- 1997
- 2006 quarter 2 (provisional)

Ethnicity	1997	2006 quarter 2 (provisional)
White	76.6%	75%
African/Caribbean	6.8%	9.5%
Indian/Pakistani/Bangladeshi	4.7%	5.4%
Other ethnic origin	5.1%	5.1%
Ethnic origin not known	6.9%	4.9%

1. Households found to be eligible for assistance, unintentionally homeless and falling within a priority need group, and consequently owed a main homelessness duty by a local housing authority. Figures reflect decisions under the 1996 Housing Act, and any residual 1985 Housing Act cases.
Totals may not equal the sum of components because of rounding.

Source: CDLG P1E Homelessness returns (quarterly).

skills) nor social networks to enable them to live independently.

During the interviews, homeless people frequently reported how engagement in learning and skills activities had helped them to restore or develop confidence and self-esteem and that this not only encouraged them to learn more, but also had a much wider impact by encouraging them to plan for a better life. This need to develop self-esteem applies to all types of homeless learners, including those who have previously had very 'successful' lives.

More than half of all homeless people want to engage in learning and skills development but only a fifth do at present

---

The interviews with homeless people revealed the loss of dignity and self-worth that accompany homelessness, and the importance of ensuring that a flexible range of learning opportunities is offered to homeless people to give them a chance to achieve – and thereby build confidence and self-esteem – within their own individual capabilities.

Several studies have confirmed that homeless people themselves also recognise the wide-ranging benefits that participation in learning and skills can give them. The majority of homeless people want to engage in learning and skills development, and yet only a fifth do so at present.

Only a third of agencies providing housing-related support to homeless people also offer support to engage in wider activities like learning. Research has shown that those who have been homeless for the longest period are much less likely to engage in learning, hence the importance of ensuring that assessment of the need for learning and encouragement of its take-up is addressed at the outset of contact with the individual by homelessness agencies.

Key findings

⇨ Investment in learning and skills work with homeless people delivers a wide range of benefits which helps to tackle their homelessness, social exclusion and deprivation and should therefore be central to the Government's homelessness strategy.

⇨ The Government recognises the important role that learning and skills play in enabling lasting solutions to homelessness, yet its delivery to homeless people is ad hoc and largely uncoordinated at present.

⇨ Despite the role that life skills training plays in enabling homeless people to progress to more independent living, the amount of Supporting People funding being used to support its delivery is being cut by administering authorities.

⇨ More than half of all homeless people want to engage in learning and skills development but only a fifth do at present.

⇨ Crisis is the national charity for single homeless people. Its mission is

to fight homelessness and empower people to fulfil their potential and transform their lives. For more information, please visit the Crisis website at www.crisis.org.uk

© Crisis

Hard work for homeless people

Information from St Mungo's

Introduction

St Mungo's surveyed 100 homeless people to identify the problems they face getting a job. Twenty years ago (1986) St Mungo's conducted a survey of homeless people, and revealed that 83% had some form of paid employment. St Mungo's reveals, 9 September 2005, that less than 5% have paid employment.

St Mungo's works with the most vulnerable people within the UK, and offers the best chance to leave a life of homelessness behind and gain employment.

Problems finding/retaining work

St Mungo's asked 100 homeless people what problems prevented them from finding work:

⇨ 2 in 3 said that agencies and employers weren't willing to give them a chance while they were homeless.

⇨ 2 in 3 said that they didn't have enough money for appropriate work clothes or work-related equipment.

⇨ 1 in 2 said they needed some help and advice but there just wasn't anyone who would help them.

⇨ 1 in 2 said they had problems getting a job without a current mailing address.

⇨ 1 in 4 stated that they had had problems due to substance use issues, mental or physical health problems.

⇨ 3 in 5 said they didn't have the right qualifications, the right work experience or any job references.

⇨ 4 in 5 said that they didn't have enough money to carry them until their first salary.

⇨ 3 in 5 said they couldn't find a job that would pay them enough for their rent and bills.

⇨ 1 in 5 said they had problems reading and writing.

St Mungo's
Opening doors for London's homeless

⇨ 1 in 4 of those surveyed are from outside London.

St Mungo's asked 50 homeless people who use its employment and training services about their experience.

Employment history

Homeless people were asked, prior to being involved with St Mungo's, when they were last employed, why they left that job and the longest period they had held the job:

⇨ 2 in 5 respondents said they hadn't had a job for at least 2 years.

⇨ 1 in 10 said they hadn't had a job for over 5 years.

⇨ 3 in 5 said they had previously held steady jobs for over 2 years.

⇨ 4 in 5 had previously held steady jobs for over a year.

Changes and looking forward

Homeless people were then asked what their ideal job was. The jobs homeless people stated they most wanted were all in areas where there are currently labour shortages in the UK:

⇨ Maintenance, building, plumbing and related jobs.

⇨ Factory and warehouse jobs.

⇨ Care and support work.

⇨ Computers and IT.

⇨ Horticulture.

⇨ Leisure industry jobs.

Homeless people were asked what they had gained from taking part in employment and employment training programmes at St Mungo's:

⇨ 4 in 5 felt they were learning new skills by being linked into the service.

⇨ 4 in 5 felt their confidence and self-esteem had increased since linking into the service.

⇨ 4 in 5 said their job finding skills had improved.

⇨ 4 in 5 had been applying for more jobs since linking into the service.

⇨ 2 in 3 were positive that their involvement would lead to them getting work.

⇨ 1 in 2 said their housing situation had improved since coming to the service.

⇨ 1 in 2 had been offered work already.

⇨ 1 in 2 felt their health had improved.

New solutions helping homeless people back to work

St Mungo's offers pioneering solutions to help homeless people back on their feet. These include:

⇨ Employment Link: The only project in the country that helps homeless people once they actually start work in their new job.

⇨ The Clothes Store: This scheme ensures that homeless people have the clothes they need for interviews and also provides clothes for clients who have started their job but are waiting for their first pay cheque.

⇨ Placement Link: This project recruits employers who provide work placements and, in some cases, permanent jobs for homeless men and women.

⇨ The Workshop: This scheme offers paid employment with staff support to aid homeless people's transition back into the world of work by teaching woodworking skills to build furniture, making sales worth over £25,000 a year.

⇨ Volunteering: Putting Down Roots is St Mungo's gardening

training scheme; homeless men and women work alongside community volunteers to improve public spaces while gaining horticultural skills.

Less than 5% of those surveyed had paid employment

⇨ Voicemail4all: Voicemail for all offers homeless people a phone number and voicemail so that they can pick up messages from potential employers when they are looking for work. Voicemail for all is managed by St Mungo's on behalf of Tech4all and with the support of the LDA, Bridge House Trust, Evoxus, Teamphone, Full Employment UK and Credit-Suisse First Boston.

⇨ St Mungo's operates an employment centre and two training centres where clients can take courses, use computers, gain NVQs and other qualifications, look for jobs, improve their CV and practice for interviews.

Work

St Mungo's offers pioneering services to men and women who have complex and overlapping needs that often exclude them from mainstream services. Our work prepares people with mental health, substance use, alcohol and housing problems to move on.

Last year, our Work and Learning programme, Europe's largest directly delivered service for homeless people, helped more than 1,700 vulnerable men and women prepare for maintaining their tenancy, holding down a job, get back in touch with their family, learn to read and write and so much more.

Quotes

'I was sceptical when I first heard about the resource centre but they were very welcoming; they helped me get a CV together, learn new work skills and apply for jobs. And now I have a job.'

'The employment team helped me realise what I want in life. I'm now totally focused on getting a job, saving money and moving on, and I've learnt not to be disappointed if things don't go my way first time.'

'The employment centre has helped me structure my job hunting. I come in for three hours a day and the atmosphere is really positive -I've met lots of new people and got my confidence back.'

'A few years ago I'd never even touched a computer – now I've got a computer qualification which means I've got a better chance of finding a job.'

⇨ The above information is reprinted with kind permission from St Mungo's. Visit www.mungos.org for more information.

© St Mungo's

The Big Issue

About the magazine

The Big Issue Magazine is a combination of hard-hitting current affairs journalism and critical, incisive writing about the world of arts and entertainment. Its high standard of reporting has won the magazine a brace of high-profile media awards.

The inspiration for the magazine came from *Street News*, a newspaper sold by homeless people in New York, which Gordon Roddick of The Body Shop saw on a visit to the States. With the assistance of The Body Shop International, Roddick and A. John Bird launched *The Big Issue* in September 1991, initially as a monthly publication in London.

In June 1993, *The Big Issue* went weekly, and regional sister titles were later established in Manchester (*The Big Issue in the North*), Glasgow (*The Big Issue Scotland*) and Cardiff (*The Big Issue Cymru*), Bristol (*The Big Issue South West*) and Birmingham (*The Big Issue Mid-lands*). Subsequently editions were also launched in Sydney – Australia, Cape Town – South Africa and Los Angeles – USA. *The Big Issue* is a founder member of the International Network of Street Papers (INSP), which links up similar magazines from all over the world.

The Big Issue campaigns on behalf of homeless and socially excluded people. It is not part of any other media group, and guards its independence fiercely. It has no party political allegiance.

Since 1996, when George Michael broke his silence to talk exclusively to the magazine, *The Big Issue* has become renowned for its exclusive celebrity interviews – stars from The Spice Girls and Kate Moss to Arnold Schwarzenegger and David Beckham have all been profiled in its pages. Guest editors have included artist Damien Hirst and author Irvine Welsh. *The Big Issue* also conducts major interviews with key political figures.

Getting results

Since The Big Issue Foundation was established in 1995, we have met and worked together with a total of 5,398 people...

⇨ 400+ vendors currently sell *The Big Issue* magazine that is distributed in London, the South East, the South West and the Midlands

⇨ 407 have gone into further education or attended a course

⇨ 281 have been rehoused

⇨ 75 have been helped into permanent employment

Source: The Big Issue

Another unique feature of the magazine is Street Lights, the only public forum for homeless people's writing in the media.

⇨ The above information is reprinted with kind permission from *The Big Issue*. Visit www.bigissue.com for more information.

© *Big Issue*

Emmaus communities

Frequently asked questions about Emmaus

Emmaus Communities offer homeless men and women a home, work and the chance to rebuild their self-respect in a supportive, community environment.
Companions, as residents are known, work full time refurbishing donated furniture and household goods and selling them in the Community shop. The Community aims to become self-sufficient through this activity.

When did Emmaus start?

The first Emmaus Community was founded in Paris in 1949 by Abbé Pierre, a priest, MP and former member of the French resistance. The idea spread around the world, but Emmaus didn't arrive in the UK until 1992, when the first Community opened in Cambridge.

What does the word 'Emmaus' mean?

The name Emmaus (pronounced e-may-us) was chosen by Abbé Pierre as it symbolises hope. It comes from a story in St Luke's Gospel and although Emmaus is not a religious organisation, Communities around the world have kept the name because of its symbolism. The story (Chapter 24, vv 13-35) describes how shortly after Jesus' death two of his followers were at Emmaus, a place near Jersualem, when they saw the resurrected Jesus and so regained hope.

What is a Companion?

Companions are the residents of Emmaus Communities, all of whom work on the Community business.

Who comes to Emmaus?

Most Emmaus Companions have been living on the streets and sleeping rough. They come from many different backgrounds and have become homeless for a variety of reasons – relationship breakdown, job loss or bereavement have often played a significant part. Many struggle with alcohol and drug dependency. Those coming to Emmaus must be prepared to work and to sign off Job Seeker's Allowance. Those addicted to alcohol or drugs must want to overcome this, as no alcohol or drugs are allowed in Communities. Many Companions find the security and support they need to face up to these problems within a Community environment.

What is Community life like?

Life at each Community varies, depending on size, location etc. However, they all work broadly in the same way. Emmaus Communities live as a family, with members supporting each other and contributing to the well-being of all. Each Companion has their own room, but meals are eaten together. Housework is shared and social events are organised, though these are not compulsory.

Communities aim to be a home, not an institution, so there are few rules. However, all Companions are required to consider the needs of others. Those breaking rules are excluded from Emmaus Communities for a period of time. All Companions work full time on the Community business to the best of their ability, refurbishing and re-selling donated furniture.

How long do people stay in a Community?

There is no limit to how long people stay in a Community – it can be anything from a couple of weeks to several years. For some, Emmaus will fill a short-term need, for example to recover from addiction, to regain their self-esteem, or to gain new skills. These people may move on to other accommodation, jobs etc. Others will stay in Emmaus for a longer time – for some it will be a permanent home. Communities benefit from having long-term Companions as they provide stability and can help and support newer Companions.

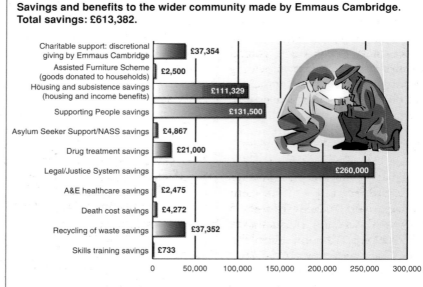

Savings made by one Emmaus community

Savings and benefits to the wider community made by Emmaus Cambridge. Total savings: £613,382.

Charitable support: discretional giving by Emmaus Cambridge	£37,354
Assisted Furniture Scheme (goods donated to households)	£2,500
Housing and subsistence savings (housing and income benefits)	£111,329
Supporting People savings	£131,500
Asylum Seeker Support/NASS savings	£4,867
Drug treatment savings	£21,000
Legal/Justice System savings	£260,000
A&E healthcare savings	£2,475
Death cost savings	£4,272
Recycling of waste savings	£37,352
Skills training savings	£733

Note: Discretional giving figures are actual for the accounting period 2001/02.

Source: Emmaus in the UK: Building on Success, Emmaus.

How does someone join an Emmaus Community?

Each Community deals with admission of new Companions independently. If somebody wishes to join they need to contact a particular Community to find out about joining that Community and whether there is a space there.

How do Emmaus Communities start?

Emmaus Communities start when a group of local people decide that a Community would benefit their area. With the support of the Emmaus UK Office, they find a site, which must provide accommodation for Companions and is also suitable for running the business. They also need to raise the money. It requires a huge amount of time and commitment from the local committee, the support of local people and about £1.5 million to start a Community, and usually takes around 2 years.

Emmaus Communities aim to become financially self-sufficient through their business

What is the structure of Emmaus in the UK?

Emmaus UK is a Federation, made up of Communities and Groups. All Communities and some Groups are independent registered charities. The Emmaus UK Office is the central office of the Federation, providing support services to Communities and Groups. It is also a registered charity.

Where does Emmaus get its money from?

Emmaus Communities aim to become financially self-sufficient through their business. It takes 5 years on average for a Community to become self-sufficient, so until this time, Communities require support from donations and grants. Groups working to set up Communities also rely on fundraising for the money to acquire a site, build/convert

accommodation and set up the business. The Emmaus UK Office fundraising team helps newer Communities and Groups in their fundraising, as well as raising money to pay for the other support services provided centrally.

I've got some furniture I don't need any more. Does Emmaus want it?

Emmaus Communities rely on donated goods to make their living, by refurbishing and reselling them. This provides work for the Companions and each Community aims to become self-sufficient through their work. However, there are some limitations on what Communities can take, depending, for example on what they can sell, how much storage space they have etc. Communities can collect items from their local area. To find out if your local Community can take a particular item or to arrange collection, please phone their shop.

⇨ The above information is reprinted with kind permission from Emmaus UK and was up to date as of 18 September 2006. Please visit www.emmaus.org.uk for more information.

© Emmaus UK

Leanne's story

Information from Emmaus UK

Two years ago I had my own home and was living with my then fiance and training to be a nurse. But with the stress of the job I started drinking and I had a problem. I started taking days off, then I couldn't pay the bills. My fiance and I split up and I went to the council because I was homeless.

The shelter I was put in was awful. There were needles in the showers and the mattress was wet with urine. It was chaos there and felt safer to sleep on the beach.

But at Emmaus I have security and continuity. They have helped me through my problems and the people here have offered me so much support and friendship.

I am starting a French course and Emmaus are paying for me to learn to drive. And I'm engaged to one of the Companions, Alan.

I feel physically sick when I think of people out on the streets with nothing and nobody. Most people on the streets would rather die than be there. There are not enough places like Emmaus and we cannot help everybody. At this Community we only have 16 beds.

⇨ The above information is reprinted with kind permission from Emmaus UK and was up to date as of 18 September 2006. Visit www.emmaus.org.uk for more information.

© Emmaus UK

⇨ People who experience homelessness are often amongst the most vulnerable people in our society, suffering from a combination of poor housing, unemployment, low income, bad health, poor skills, loneliness, isolation and relationship breakdown. (page 1)

⇨ Crisis estimates that there are around 380,000 single homeless people in Great Britain, including those staying in hostels, B&Bs, squats, on friends' floors and overcrowded accommodation. (page 2)

⇨ For as long as historical records have been kept, Britain has had a homelessness problem. As far back as the 7th century, the English king Hlothaere passed laws to punish vagrants. It was in the 16th century that the state first tried to house vagrants rather than punish them. (page 4)

⇨ Only a tiny proportion of homeless people are on the street. Most stay on friends' floors or with family, sometimes in precarious arrangements that can go wrong. (page 7)

⇨ The latest government figures estimate that there are 459 people sleeping rough on any given night in England. Of these, nearly 50 per cent sleep rough in London. A report for the Office of the Deputy Prime Minister, however, has acknowledged that the number of people sleeping rough over the course of a year is at least ten times higher than the snapshot on any given night provided by the street counts. (page 10)

⇨ Around half of people sleeping rough have either been in prison or to a young offenders' institution, and many have had repeated contact with the police and courts. (page 11)

⇨ Research has found that female sex workers form one of the most excluded and marginalised groups of homeless people. (page 12)

⇨ Around 25 per cent of rough sleepers are aged between 18 and 25, and six per cent are over 60. (page 14)

⇨ Young people who become homeless are more likely to have lived with stepparents, foster parents or relatives by the age of 12 than those who do not become homeless. (page 15)

⇨ The Government has committed to increasing the rate of house building to 200,000 new homes each year by 2016 to address the supply and affordability problems. (page 16)

⇨ Migrants, refugees and asylum seekers can be especially vulnerable to homelessness. (page 19)

⇨ About half of people sleeping rough are heavy drinkers and about one in seven are drug addicts. (page 20)

⇨ The rate of tuberculosis among rough sleepers and hostel residents is 200 times that of the known rate among the general population. (page 20)

⇨ There are a number of reasons why young people become homeless. Family and relationship breakdowns are the most common factor. (page 21)

⇨ Young homeless people are also likely to miss up to a quarter of their schooling. (page 21)

⇨ One in 12 young people are more likely to get sick because of bad housing and are more likely to be injured due to badly designed homes or dangerous fittings. (page 23)

⇨ Shelter estimates that over one million children in Britain are living in housing that damages their health, their education and their future. (page 23)

⇨ Eighty-two per cent of homeless young people surveyed by Centrepoint were in debt, owing £1,000 on average, but as much as £15,000 in one case. (page 24)

⇨ A number of homeless young people surveyed by Centrepoint owe money to friends or relatives – 37%, compared to 6% of the total population. (page 26)

⇨ Over two-thirds (69%) of the young homeless people aged 16-25 surveyed by the Mental Health Foundation have mental health problems. (page 27)

⇨ The services for people sleeping on the streets are based mainly in cities and large towns. Rural areas also have services, but they may be more limited. (page 31)

⇨ 37% of homeless people surveyed by Crisis for their 'Missed Opportunities' report have no qualifications (compared to 10% of general population). (page 34)

⇨ 400+ vendors currently sell the *Big Issue* magazine that is distributed in London, the South East, the South West and the Midlands. (page 37)

⇨ Emmaus Communities offer homeless men and women a home, work and the chance to rebuild their self-respect in a supportive, community environment. Companions, as residents are known, work full time refurbishing donated furniture and household goods and selling them in the community shop. The community aims to become self-sufficient through this activity. (page 38)

GLOSSARY

Begging

A beggar is a homeless person who makes money by asking for donations from passers-by. Although begging and homelessness are inextricably linked, not all rough sleepers beg or vice versa. However, the vast majority of those who beg are in unstable accommodation. Research found that only six individuals, out of a sample of 260 people who beg, were living in their own home.

The Big Issue

A weekly magazine sold by homeless people in the UK. Launched in 1995, the money made from magazine sales is used to benefit homeless people.

Day shelters

Day centres are places that people sleeping on the streets can go to during the day. People who have left the streets can also use them for activities and companionship even if they are living in their own homes.

Hidden homelessness

The problem of single people who exist out of sight in hostels, bed and breakfasts, squats or with friends and family. These homeless people are often not identified by government statistics, and are hidden from view. It is said to affect around 4,000 people in Britain and is most common in people aged 16 to 25.

Homeless households

A family or individual who has applied for local authority housing support and been judged to be homeless.

Homelessness

In its broadest sense homelessness is the problem faced by people who lack a place to live that is supportive, affordable, decent and secure. Whilst rough sleepers are the most visible homeless population, the vast majority of homeless people live in hostels, squats, bed and breakfasts or in temporary and insecure conditions with friends and family.

Hostels and nightshelters

Hostels and nightshelters provide housing for people sleeping on the streets.

Outreach teams

In some areas known as Contact and Assessment Teams (CATs). These groups work on the street, advising people how to find accommodation.

Priority need

Under the homeless legislation certain categories of homeless household are considered to have priority need for accommodation. Priority need applies to families with dependent children, and households that include someone who is vulnerable due to pregnancy, old age, physical disability, mental illness or domestic violence.

Resettlement teams

Some hostels may have a resettlement worker or team; they can help to find longer-term housing.

Rough sleeping

A rough sleeper is a homeless person who is literally 'roofless' and lives predominantly on the streets. Government figures, based on street counts, suggest that there are 459 people sleeping rough on any given night in England.

Single homeless

This term refers to homeless individuals or couples without dependants.

Soup runs

In some areas, agencies distribute free food and drinks to people sleeping on the streets.

Statutory homelessness

Refers to those homeless people or households who are recognised by local authorities to be homeless and are therefore recognised in government homeless statistics.

Street homelessness

Often confused with rough sleeping, street homelessness is actually a much wider term, also taking into account the street lifestyles of some people who may not actually sleep on the streets.

INDEX